THE RICHEST PERSON IN BABYLON

REVISED FOR MODERN TIMES

GEORGE S. CLASON

EDITED BY
CLIFTON D. CORBIN

&

KALEB K. A. CORBIN

First published in 1926 as separate pamphlets by George S. Clason.

ISBN 978-1-7778695-4-0 (paperback)
ISBN 978-1-7778695-5-7 (ebook)

Illustrations by Matthew Holliday.

Cover Wildwinds Babylon Coin used with permission of woodwinds.com, ex D. Thomas Collection

Cover art © 2022 Patterin Publishing. All rights reserved.

Patterin Publishing • Toronto, Ontario, Canada
www.patterin.com • info@patterin.com

Quantity discounts are available to your company or institution for reselling, educational purposes, subscription incentives, gifts, or fundraiser campaigns. Contact info@patterin.com for more information.

CONTENTS

EDITORS' NOTE

The Richest Man in Babylon has been one of the most influential financial books for generations. In this updated version we attempt to give a fresh voice to this classic, and to make the parables speak to a modern reader with inclusivity and plain language. We have made the following changes to the original text to meet those objectives.

We have removed Clason's verbal flourishes while being careful not to change the lessons to be learned from the parables. The flourishes are part of Clason's unique style, but we felt that they distract a modern reader from the concepts being taught. Embellishments such as *thee*, *thou*, and *thy* have been simplified and replaced with *you* or *your*. The use of *-est* and *-eth* at the end of some verbs in the present tense has been eliminated, so that *retainest*, *thinkest*, and *earneth* are now simply *retain*, *think*, and *earn*. For example: "Which desirest thou the most?" has become "What do you desire the most?"

The original text referred to people, animals, and things with masculine pronouns. We have revised these gendered pronouns. For example, "Gold in a man's purse must be guarded with firmness, else it be lost," has been rewritten as "Gold in one's purse must be guarded with determination, or it will be lost." Moreover, to make the story more inclusive, we have changed the gender of some of the named characters. The original text included only male-named characters (with the exceptions of brief mentions of wives or female family members). An example of this shift from the original text is in the Five Laws of Gold. Arkad's son Nomasir retells his tale in the original, but in our version Nomasir has become Nomasira and is the daughter of Arkad.

One challenging word was *purse*, which was used in the original version to refer to all people's personal "bags" of coins. We generally felt that *purse* didn't flow smoothly in the text, and so we have replaced it with *wallet* or *purse and wallet* in some contexts.

A note on money: a penny is less than a shekel which is less than a copper which is less than a silver coin which is less than a gold coin.

Many sections in the text use slavery terminology when referring to money working for people and people toiling for people. We have when possible removed references to slavery when the text addresses money working for people. The original text uses the analogy of investments as "slaves to you the master, working to earn you more money." While the analogy may be apt, we feel that using the concept of slavery is unnecessary and insensitive.

Two stories in the original text use slavery as a central theme, "The Camel Trader" and the "Luckiest Man in Babylon." We didn't want to cleanse the concept of slavery from a historical sense, and in the updated story of the "Luckiest Person in Babylon" slavery remains as central to the plot. But in "The Camel Trader," we adapt the story to portray the enslaved people as prisoners who are unpaid laborers, which is more in line with how some current criminal justice systems work. Hopefully, this update will make the story more representative and relatable for a modern reader.

All of the updated parables are versions of the original text, with the exception of "The Walls of Babylon." We felt the original version of this story didn't demonstrate the core principle of securing one's wealth. We also found the story to be gruesome, with a lot of talk of death and battle. To achieve the objective of making this version universally appealing to young and old, we felt this story needed to be different. We hope the new "Walls of Babylon" better captures in an enjoyable and approachable manner the concept of protecting one's wealth.

Lastly, this version, while updated, has not been fact-checked. The historical notes in "A Historical Sketch of Babylon" were not made current based on any new findings that may have occurred since the original publication in 1926. Nor have we fact-checked the rest of the text based on any data that has come to light since then either.

We hope you enjoy this version of *The Richest Man in Babylon*. Moreover, we hope that making a more readable, more inclusive version of this classic may help it stand the test of time for another hundred years.

May the lessons outline in this book serve you well and help you to master your finances.

Clifton D. Corbin
Kaleb K. A. Corbin

FOREWORD

Our prosperity as a nation depends on the personal financial prosperity of each of us as individuals.

This book deals with the personal successes of each of us. Success means accomplishments as the result of our own efforts and abilities. Proper preparation is the key to our success. Our acts can be no wiser than our thoughts. Our thinking can be no wiser than our understanding.

This book of cures for lean purses has been termed a guide to financial understanding. That, indeed, is its purpose: to offer those who are ambitious for financial success an insight which will help them to acquire money, to keep money, and to make their surpluses earn more money.

In the pages which follow we are taken back to Babylon, the place where the basic principles of finance, now recognized and used the world over, were created and nurtured.

To new readers, the author is happy to extend the wish that its pages may contain for them the same inspiration for growing bank accounts, greater financial successes, and the solution to difficult personal financial problems so enthusiastically reported by readers from coast to coast.

To the business executives who have distributed these tales in such generous quantities to friends, relatives, employees, and associates, the author takes this opportunity to express his gratitude. No endorsement could be higher than that of practical people who appreciate its teachings because they themselves have worked up to important successes by applying the very principles it advocates.

Babylon became the wealthiest city of the ancient world because its citizens were the richest people of their time. They appreciated the value of money. They practiced sound financial principles in acquiring money, keeping money, and making their money earn more money. They provided for themselves what we all desire . . . incomes for the future.

G. S. C.

A HISTORICAL SKETCH
OF BABYLON

In the pages of history, there lives no city more glamorous than Babylon. Its very name conjures visions of wealth and splendor. Its treasures of gold and jewels were fabulous. One naturally pictures such a wealthy city as located in a suitable setting of tropical luxury, surrounded by rich natural resources of forests and mines. Such wasn't the case as Babylon was situated beside the Euphrates River in a flat, arid valley. There were no forests, no mines - not even stone for building. It wasn't even located on a natural trade route. The rainfall was insufficient to raise crops.

Babylonians are an outstanding example of humans' ability to achieve great objectives, using whatever means are at their disposal. All of the resources supporting this large city were manufactured. All of its riches were developed by people.

Babylon had just two natural resources - fertile soil and water in the river. With one of the most significant engineering accomplishments of this or any other day, Babylonian engineers diverted the waters from the river employing dams and immense irrigation canals. Far out across that arid valley went these canals to pour the life-giving waters over the fertile soil. This ranks among the first engineering feat known to history. Abundant crops were the reward of this irrigation system the world had never seen before.

Fortunately, Babylon was ruled by successive lines of kings during its long existence to whom conquest and plunder were but incidental. While it engaged in many wars, most of these were local or defensive against ambitious conquerors from other countries who coveted the fabulous treasures of Babylon. The outstanding rulers of Babylon live in history because of their wisdom, enterprise and justice. Babylon produced no strutting monarchs who sought to conquer the known world that all nations might pay homage to their egotism.

As a city, Babylon exists no more. When those energizing human forces that built and maintained the city for thousands of years were withdrawn, it soon became a deserted ruin. The city's site is in Asia, about six hundred miles east of the Suez Canal, just north of the Persian Gulf. The latitude is about thirty degrees above the Equator, practically the same as Yuma, Arizona. Consequently, it possessed a hot and dry climate similar to this American city.

Today, this valley of the Euphrates, once a populous irrigated farming district, is again a wind-swept arid waste. Scant grass and desert shrubs strive for existence against the windblown sands. Gone are the fertile fields, the mammoth cities and the long caravans of rich merchandise. Instead, nomadic peoples, securing a living by tending small herds, are the only inhabitants. Such it has been since about the beginning of the Common era.

Dotting this valley are earthen hills. For centuries, they were considered by travelers to be nothing else. Archaeologists were finally attracted to them because of broken pieces of pottery and brick washed down by the occasional rainstorms. Expeditions, financed by European and American museums, were sent here to excavate and see what could be found. Picks and shovels soon proved these hills to be ancient cities. One might call them City graves. Babylon was one of these.

Built originally of brick, all exposed walls had disintegrated and gone back to earth once more. Such is Babylon, the wealthy city today. A heap of dirt, so long abandoned that no living person even knew its name until it was discovered by carefully removing the refuse of centuries from the streets, and the fallen wreckage of its noble temples and palaces.

Many scientists consider the civilization of Babylon and other cities in this valley to be the oldest of which there is a definite record. Dates have proven to reach back 8000 years. The means used to determine these dates may be interesting to some. Uncovered in the ruins of Babylon were descriptions of an eclipse of the sun. Modern astronomers computed when such an eclipse, visible in Babylon, occurred and thus established a known relationship between their calendar and our own.

This is how its been proved that 8000 years ago the Sumerites, who inhabited Babylonia were living in walled cities. However, the inhabitants weren't "barbarians" living within protecting walls. On the contrary, they were educated and enlightened people. So far as written history goes, they were the first engineers, astronomers, mathematicians, financiers, and the first people to have a written language.

Mention has already been made of the irrigation systems which transformed the arid valley into an agricultural paradise. The remains of these canals can still be traced, although they are mostly filled with accumulated sand. Some of them were of such size that a dozen horses could be ridden abreast along their bottoms when empty of water. In size, they compared favorably with the largest canals built in Colorado and Utah during the early 20th century.

In addition to irrigating the valley lands, Babylonian engineers completed another project of similar magnitude. Using an elaborate drainage system, they reclaimed a massive area of swampland at the mouths of the Euphrates and Tigris Rivers and also put this under cultivation.

Herodotus, the Greek traveler and historian, visited Babylon while it was in its prime and gave us an outsider's only known description. His writings provide a graphic depiction of the city and some of the unusual customs of its people. He also mentions the remarkable fertility of the soil and the bountiful harvest of wheat and barley which they produced.

The glory of Babylon has faded, but its wisdom has been preserved for us. For this, we are indebted to their form of records. In that distant day, the use of paper hadn't been invented. Instead, they laboriously engraved their writing on tablets of moist clay. When completed, these were baked and became hard tile. They were about six by eight inches and an inch in thickness.

These clay tablets, as they are commonly called, were used as we use modern forms of writing. On them were engraved legends, poetry, history, transcriptions of royal decrees, the laws of the land, titles to property, promissory notes and even letters dispatched by messengers to distant cities. From these clay tablets, we are permitted an insight into the intimate, personal affairs of the people. For example, one tablet, evidently from the records of a country storekeeper, relates that on the given date, a certain named customer brought in a cow and exchanged it for seven sacks of wheat, three being delivered at the time and the other four to await the customer's pleasure.

Safely buried in the wrecked cities, archaeologists have recovered entire libraries comprising of hundreds of thousands of these tablets.

One of the incredible wonders of Babylon was the immense walls surrounding the city. The ancients ranked them with the great pyramids of Egypt as belonging to the "seven wonders of the world." Queen Semiramis is credited with having erected the first walls during the city's early history. Unfortunately, modern excavators have been unable to find any trace of the original walls. Nor are their exact heights known. However, from mention made by early writers, it's estimated they were about fifty to sixty feet high, faced on the outer side with burnt brick and further protected by a deep moat of water.

The later and more famous walls were started about six hundred years before the time of Christ by King Nabopolassar. Although he planned the rebuilding on such a gigantic scale, he didn't live to see the work finished. Instead, this was left to his son, Nebuchadnezzar, a name familiar in Biblical history.

The height and length of these later walls staggered belief. They are reported from reliable authority to have been about one hundred and sixty feet high, the equivalent of the height of a modern fifteen-story office building. The total length is estimated as between nine and eleven miles. So wide was the top that a six-horse chariot could be driven around them. Of this massive structure, little now remains except portions of the foundations and the moat. In addition to the ravages of the elements, local people completed the destruction by quarrying the brick for building purposes elsewhere.

Against the walls of Babylon marched victorious armies of almost every conqueror of that age of wars of conquest. A host of kings laid siege to Babylon but always in vain. Invading troops of that day weren't to be considered lightly. Historians speak of such units as 10,000 horsemen, 25,000 chariots, 1200 regiments of foot soldiers with 1000 to each regiment. Often two or three years of preparation would be required to assemble war materials, and depots of food along the proposed line of march.

The city of Babylon was organized much like a modern city. You would find streets and shops where peddlers offered their wares through residential districts. Priests officiated in magnificent temples. Within the city was an inner enclosure for the royal palaces. The walls about this were said to have been higher than those about the city.

The Babylonians were skilled artisans creating sculpture, painting, weaving, gold working, metal weapons and agricultural implements. Their jewelers made the most artistic jewelry. Many samples have been recovered from the site and are now on exhibition in museums worldwide.

At a very early period when the rest of the world was still hacking at trees with stone-headed axes or hunting and fighting with flint-pointed spears and arrows, the Babylonians were using axes, spears and arrows with metal tips.

The Babylonians were clever financiers and traders. So far as we know, they were one of the original inventors of money as a means of exchange, promissory notes and written titles to property.

Hostile armies never entered Babylon until about 540 years before the start of the common era. Even then, the walls weren't captured. The story of the fall of Babylon, some may say, is unusual. Cyrus, one of the great conquerors of that period, intended to attack the city and hoped to breach its impregnable walls. Advisors of Nabonidus, the King of Babylon, persuaded him to go forth to meet Cyrus and give him battle without waiting for the city to be besieged. In the successive defeat of the Babylonian army, it fled away from the city. Cyrus, thereupon, entered the open gates and took possession without resistance.

After that, the power and prestige of the city gradually waned. Until, in the course of a few hundred years, it was eventually abandoned and deserted. It was left for the wind to level it again to the desert from which it had initially been built. Babylon had fallen, never to rise again, but to it, civilization owes much.

The eons of time have crumbled to dust the proud walls of its temples, but the wisdom of Babylon endures.

Money is the medium by which worldly success is measured.

Money makes possible the enjoyment of the best the earth affords.

Money is plentiful for those who understand the simple laws which govern its acquisition.

Money is governed today by the same laws which controlled it when prosperous people thronged the streets of Babylon six thousand years ago.

CHAPTER I

THE ONE WHO DESIRED GOLD

Bansir, the chariot builder of Babylon, was thoroughly discouraged. From his seat on the low wall surrounding his property, he gazed sadly at his simple home and the open workshop in which stood a partially completed chariot.

His wife frequently appeared at the open door. Her intense glances in his direction reminded him that the cupboards were almost empty, and he should be at work finishing the chariot, hammering, polishing, painting, and stretching the leather over the wheel rims. Preparing it for delivery so he could collect from his wealthy customer.

Nevertheless, he sat calmly on the wall. His mind was struggling with a problem for which he couldn't find an answer. The hot tropical sun, so typical of this part of the world, beat down on him mercilessly. Beads of sweat formed on his brow and trickled unnoticed down his cheek and chin.

Beyond his home towered the high wall surrounding the king's palace. Nearby, distinct against the blue sky, was the tower of the Temple of Bel. In the shadow of such riches was his simple home, and many others homes that were far less neat and well cared for.

Babylon was like this — a mixture of grandeur and squalor, of dazzling wealth and the lowest poverty, crowded together without plan or system within the protection of the city walls.

Behind him, if he cared to turn around, he would see and hear the noisy chariots of the rich rolling along the crowded streets full of tradespeople and the barefooted poor. Even the rich were forced to clear the way for the long lines of water carriers' servants on the "king's business," each carrying a heavy sack of water to be poured on the hanging gardens.

Bansir was too absorbed in his own problem to hear or notice the confused noise of the busy city. It was the unexpected strumming of the strings from a familiar guitar that pulled him out of his trance. He turned and looked into the sensitive, smiling face of his best friend — Kobbi, the musician.

"May the Gods bless you with great prosperity, my good friend," began Kobbi with an elaborate salute. "Although it seems as if they have already granted their favor on you. You must be doing well for yourself, sitting here idle in the middle of the day with no need to work. I am grateful for your good fortune and a bit jealous. Could you do me the smallest favor and lend me a few silver coins, old friend? I am low on funds. I only need them for a few days, just until I can perform at the feast tomorrow night. You surely wouldn't miss a few coins."

"If I had a few extra coins," Bansir responded gloomily, "there is no one I would trust more than you to lend them to. Unfortunately, I don't even have enough to go to the market, and definitely not enough to lend to my oldest friend. If I lent you a coin, it would be my fortune — my entire fortune. No one can lend their entire fortune, not even to his best friend."

"What?" exclaimed Kobbi with genuine surprise. "You don't even have a coin to lend, yet you sit like a statue on the wall! Why don't you finish that chariot? How else can you pay for all that you need and all that you want? This isn't like you, my friend. Where is your endless energy? Did something happen? You don't look injured.

What is bothering you? Why do you seem so down? Please, friend, tell me, why have the Gods troubled you?"

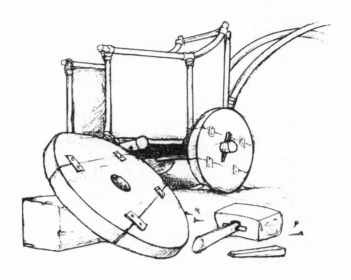

"My stress must be from the Gods," Bansir agreed. "It began with a dream, a senseless dream, in which I thought I was rich. My pockets were filled with heavy coins of gold and silver. I spent my money with careless freedom. I gave to the poor and the shopkeepers. I spent my silver buying my partner and myself whatever we desired. Fine clothing and the ripest fruit you've ever seen. In addition to the silver, I had gold hidden safely away, which made me feel that my future was secure, and I didn't need to worry about spending the silver. A glorious feeling of contentment was within me! You wouldn't have recognized me as your hardworking friend. Nor would you recognize my wife, so free of worry and anxiety, her face shone with happiness as it did when we were first married."

"A pleasant dream, indeed," commented Kobbi, "but why would such pleasant feelings turn you into a depressed statue on the wall?"

"Why, indeed! Because when I woke up and remembered how empty my pockets were, a feeling of defiance swept over me. Let's talk about this for a moment since the two of us are very much alike. As youngsters, we went to the same teachers to learn wisdom. As youths, we hung out together. As adults, we've always been close friends. We've been happy to work long hours and spend our earnings freely. We've earned many coins in the years that have passed, yet to know the joys that come from wealth, we must dream about them. Bah! Aren't we no more than dumb sheep? We live in the richest city in the world. The travelers say no other city equals it in wealth. We can see this wealth and riches on display all around us, but we have none of it! After half a lifetime of hard work, you, my best friend, have an empty wallet and say to me, 'May I borrow a few coins, a pittance, until after the nobles' feast in a night?'

"Then, what do I reply? Do I say, 'Here is my wallet. Take whatever you need, I am happy to share'? No, I admit that my pockets are as empty as yours. What is the matter? Why can't we acquire silver and gold – more than enough for food and clothes?

"Think about our children and our children's children," Bansir continued. "Are they not following in our footsteps? They too will live in this rich city, yet they are forced to be happy with water and to feast on porridge."

"Never, in all of our years of friendship, have you talked like this before, Bansir." Kobbi was puzzled.

"Never in all those years did I *think* like this before. From early dawn and until darkness stopped me, I have worked to build the finest chariots any man could make, secretly hoping that someday the Gods would recognize my worthy deeds and bestow upon me great prosperity. This they have never done. I realize, finally, that they never will. This is why my heart is sad. I want to be a person of means. I want to own lands and cattle, to have fine clothes and money in my wallet. I am willing to work for these things with all the strength in my back, with all the skill in my hands, with all the cunning in my mind, but I want my labors to be fairly rewarded.

What is the matter with us? Again I ask you! Why can't we have our fair share of the good things that are so plentiful for the rich people who have the gold to buy them?"

"I wish I knew an answer!" Kobbi replied. "I am no better than you. My earnings from my music are gone as quickly as I make them. Often I have to plan and scheme so that my family won't go hungry. Also, within my soul is a deep longing for the perfect instrument, crafted so well that it could play as well as the music I hear in my mind. I could make music finer than even the king has heard before with such an instrument."

"You should have such an instrument, and no one in all Babylon would make it sing more sweetly than you. So sweetly that not only the king but the Gods themselves would be delighted. But how may I ask are you to acquire it while we both as poor today as we were on our first days at work? Listen to the bell! Here they come."

Bansir pointed to the long column of sweating water bearers, plodding slowly up the narrow street from the river. They marched side by side, each bent under a heavy sack of water.

"The leader is a fine figure." Kobbi indicated the wearer of the bell, who marched in front without a load of water. "He is important in his own country. It's easy to see."

"There are many good people in that line," Bansir agreed, "as good as we are. All marching together from the river to the gardens, back and forth, day after day, year after year. No happiness to look forward to. Beds of straw on which to sleep – hard grain porridge to eat. Pity the poor souls, Kobbi!"

"I do pity them. Yet, you do make me see how little better off *we* are, even though we call ourselves free."

"That's true, Kobbi, as unpleasant a thought as it might be. We don't want to go on year after year, living servile lives. Working, working, working! Getting nowhere."

"Maybe . . . maybe we could find out how others acquire gold and keep it as they do?" Kobbi inquired.

"Perhaps there is some secret we might learn if we seek out those who know it," replied Bansir thoughtfully.

"Today," suggested Kobbi, "I passed our old friend, Arkad, riding in his golden chariot. But, I'll say this much, he didn't look past me as many with his wealth might. Instead, he waved at me in front of everyone. He even gave me a warm greeting and a friendly smile."

"He is said to be the richest person in all Babylon," Bansir said.

"So rich that the king is said to seek his assistance in the money affairs of the kingdom," Kobbi replied.

"So rich," Bansir interrupted, "I think if I ran into him in the darkness of the night, I would reach for his fat wallet."

"Don't be ridiculous," admonished Kobbi. "A person's wealth isn't in the wallet they carry. A fat wallet empties quickly if there is no stream of gold to refill it. Arkad has an income that constantly keeps his wallet full, no matter how much he spends."

"Income, that's the thing," exclaimed Bansir. "I want an income that will keep flowing into my wallet whether I sit on my wall or travel to distant countries. Arkad must know how to make an income for himself. Do you think it's something he could make clear to someone as simple as me?"

"I think he taught his daughter, Nomasira," Kobbi responded. "Didn't his daughter go to Nineveh? People say that without any help from her father, she became one of the richest citizens in that city."

"Kobbi, I have an idea." A new light gleamed in Bansir's eyes. "It costs nothing to ask wise advice from a good friend, and Arkad was always that. Who cares if our wallets are as empty as my pantry shelves? We won't let that deter us. We are tired of not having any gold in the midst of plenty. We want to become people of means. Let's go to Arkad and ask how we can get incomes for ourselves too."

"What you say is an inspiration, Bansir. You've made me rethink. It's only now I realize why we've never found any amount of wealth: we've never tried to get it. You've worked tirelessly to build the best chariots in Babylon. You spent all your energy reaching that goal.

That is what you succeeded in doing. I worked to become a skillful musician. And that's what I've become."

"In the things we devoted our energy to, we succeeded. The Gods were content to let us continue like this. Now, at last, we see the light, bright as the rising sun. It calls us to learn more so that we'll prosper more. With a new understanding, we'll find honest ways to accomplish our goals."

"Let's go to Arkad today," Bansir urged. "And let's ask other old friends, who have done no better than we have, to come with us so that they can receive his wisdom too."

"You have always been a good friend, thinking of others and their needs. That's why you have so many friends, Bansir. So, yes, let's go today and take them with us."

CHAPTER 2

THE RICHEST PERSON IN BABYLON

In old Babylon, there once lived a very rich man named Arkad. Far and wide, he was known for his great wealth and was famous for his generosity. Generous in giving. Generous with his family. He spent liberally on himself, but still each year his wealth increased faster than he spent it.

One day a group of old friends from Arkad's youth came to him and said: "Arkad, you are more fortunate than we are. You have become the richest person in all Babylon while we struggle every day just to survive. You wear the finest clothes and enjoy the best foods while we are just barely able to clothe and feed our families at all.

"Yet we were once equal. We studied under the same teachers. We played the same games. And in neither school nor our games did you outperform us. As far as we can tell, you haven't worked harder or more diligently than we have. Why, then, do the Gods single you out to be lucky to enjoy all the good things of life and ignore us who are just as deserving?"

At that point, Arkad scolded them, saying, "If you haven't acquired more than the bare minimum in all the years since we were kids, it's because you either have failed to learn the laws for building wealth, or you don't follow them. Luck has nothing to do with my success.

"What the Gods give with one hand they happily take away with the other. Luck doesn't stay with anyone for long. Those who use luck to gain gold almost always bring ruin on themselves. They are careless and easy spenders. And when they are inevitably faced with wants that are beyond their means, they are tormented, because they don't have the ability to earn more gold to satisfy their desires.

"Then there are those who gain riches through luck and become hoarders. They stockpile their gold, afraid to spend any of what they have because they know they don't have the ability to replace it. They live in fear of loss, by robbers or by their own desires, and doom themselves to lives in secret misery.

"There are probably others who can take unearned gold, add to it, and continue to be happy and contented citizens. But they are so few, I know of them only from rumors. Just think of those who have inherited sudden wealth and see if I am mistaken."

His friends admitted that these words were true of the people they knew who had inherited wealth. They asked him to explain to them how he had come into possession of so much prosperity, so he continued.

"When I was young, I looked around and saw all the good things there were to bring happiness and contentment. And I realized that wealth was the key to achieving of all them. Wealth is power. With wealth, many things are possible.

"You may decorate your home with fine furniture. You may travel abroad. You may feast on the delicacies of the cuisines of other countries. You may buy statues and fine art. You may even build mighty temples for the Gods. You may do all these things and many others that can be a delight for the senses and gratification for the soul.

"And when I realized all this, I decided that I would claim my share of the good things of life. I wouldn't be one of those who stand off to the side, enviously watching others enjoy. I wouldn't be content in the cheapest clothes. I wouldn't be satisfied to live a life of just getting by. No, I would have the good things.

"As the son of a humble merchant and one child of a large family with no hope of an inheritance – and, as you have said so frankly, with no superior power or wisdom – I decided that to achieve all that I wanted, it would require time and study.

"We all have time in abundance. Each of you has let enough time slip by to have made yourselves wealthy. Yet, you admit, you haven't achieved anything except your good families, of which you should be proud.

"As for study, didn't our wise teacher tell us that there are two kinds of learning? First, the things we learned and know, and second, the ability to find out what we don't know?

"Therefore I decided to find out how someone might accumulate wealth. And once I found out how, I would make it my goal and do it well. Shouldn't we enjoy the beauty of this world while our eyes can still see the brightness of the sun? As we all know, our time in this world is limited.

"I found work as a record-keeper in the hall of records, and I carved on clay tablets for long hours each day. Week after week, and month after month, I worked, yet I had nothing to show for my earnings. Food, clothing, offerings to the Gods, and other small things I don't remember absorbed all my earnings. But my determination didn't leave me.

"And one day Farida, the moneylender, came to the hall of records and ordered a copy of the Ninth Law. She said to me, 'I must have this in two days, and if the work is done by that time, I will pay you two coppers.'

"So I worked hard, but the law was long, and when Farida returned, the task was unfinished. She was angry, and if I had been her employee, she would have fired me. But knowing my boss wouldn't let me go, I wasn't afraid, so I said to her, 'Farida, you are very rich. Tell me how I may also become rich, and I will carve this clay all night, and when the sun rises, the work will be done.'

"She smiled at me and replied, 'You are a bold rascal, but we will call it a deal.'

"I carved all night. I carved even though my back hurt. The smell of the burning candles made my head ache until I could hardly see. But when she returned at sun up, the tablets were complete.

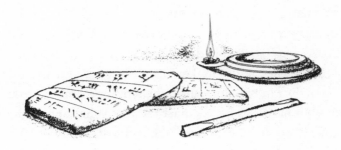

"'Now,' I said, 'tell me what you promised.'

"'You have fulfilled your part of our deal,' she said to me kindly, 'and I am ready to fulfill mine. I will tell you what you want to know because I am old, and old tongues love to talk. And when a youth comes to the old for advice, they receive the wisdom of many years. But too often, the young think that the old only know the wisdom of the past and have nothing of value to offer. But remember: the sun that shines today is the sun that shone when your ancestors were born and will still be shining when your last grandchild passes into the darkness.

"'The thoughts of the young,' she continued, 'are bright lights that shine forth like the meteors that often make the sky brilliant, but the wisdom of the old is like the fixed stars that shine so constantly that the sailor may depend on them to steer their course.

"'Remember my words because if you don't, you will fail to grasp the truth that I will tell you, and you will think that your night's work has been in vain.'

"Then she looked at me shrewdly from under her grey eyebrows and said in a low, forceful tone, 'I found the road to wealth when I decided that a part of all I earned was mine to keep. And so will you.'

"She continued to look at me with a glance that I could feel pierce me but said no more.

"'Is that all?' I asked.

"'That was sufficient to change the heart of a shepherd into the heart of a moneylender,' she replied.

"'But *all* I earn is mine to keep, isn't it?' I asked.

"'Far from it,' she replied. 'Don't you pay the garment maker? Don't you pay the sandal maker? Don't you pay for the things you eat? Can you live in Babylon without spending? What do you have to show for your earnings for the past month? What about for the past year? Fool! You pay to everyone but yourself. You work for others. You might as well be the servant to all of Babylon and work for what the store owners give you to eat and wear out of pity.

"'Let me ask you this: if you kept for yourself one-tenth of all you earn, how much would you have in ten years?'

"My knowledge of math didn't fail me, and I answered, 'As much as I earn in one year.'

"'You are only half right,' she retorted. 'Every gold piece you save is a servant to work for you. Every copper it earns is its servant that can also earn for you. If you want to become wealthy, what you *save* must earn, and what you *earn* must earn. Only in doing so will all of your savings help give you the wealth you crave.

"'I can see you think I have cheated you for your long night's work,' she continued, 'but I am paying you a thousand times more than any copper or gold if you have the intelligence to grasp the truth I offer you.

"'A part of all you earn is yours to keep. It should never be less than a tenth no matter how little you make, but it can be as much as you can afford. Pay yourself first. Don't buy from the tailor and the sandal maker more than you can pay using the rest of your earnings and still have enough for food, charity, and penance to the Gods.

"'Wealth, like a tree, grows from a tiny seed. The first coin you save is the seed from which your tree of wealth will grow. The sooner you plant that seed, the sooner the tree will grow. And the more faithfully you nourish and water that tree with consistent savings, the sooner you will be able to bask in its shade.'

"After saying that, she took her tablets and went away.

"I thought a lot about what she had said to me, and it seemed reasonable. So I decided that I would try it. Each time I was paid, I took one from every ten pieces of copper and hid it away. As strange as it may seem, I didn't seem to have any less funds than before. I noticed little difference as I managed to get along without what I saved. But I was often tempted, as my savings began to grow, to spend it for some of the good things the merchants displayed. But I wisely refrained.

"A year after Farida had gone, she again returned and said to me, 'So, have you paid yourself not less than one-tenth of all you have earned for the past year?'

"I answered proudly, 'Yes, I have.'

"'That's good,' she answered with a twinkle in her eye, 'and what have you done with it?'

"'I have given it to Azmur, the brick maker, who is travelling over the far seas. In Tyre, he will buy rare Phoenician jewels. We will sell these jewels at high prices and divide the earnings when he returns.'

"'Every fool must learn,' she growled, 'but why would you trust the knowledge of a brick maker about jewels? Would you go to the bread maker to ask about the stars? No, by goodness, you would go to the astronomer if you had the power to think. Your savings are gone. You have pulled up your wealth-tree up by the roots. But plant another one. Try again. And next time if you want advice about jewels, go to the jeweler. If you want to know about sheep, go to the shepherd. Advice is one thing that's given away freely but be careful that you take only what is worth having. Someone who takes advice about their investments from someone who is inexperienced will use their savings to prove what is fact and fiction.' Saying this, she went away.

"And Farida's predictions were right. The Phoenicians were cheats and sold to Azmur worthless bits of glass that looked like gems. But as Farida had instructed me, I again saved each tenth copper, since it was now a habit and no longer difficult.

"Twelve months later, Farida came to the hall of records and greeted me. 'What progress have you made since last I saw you?'

"'I have paid myself faithfully,' I replied, 'and I have given my savings to Aaliyah the shield maker to buy bronze. She uses the bronze to make fine shields and pays me every four months in coppers and silver for the use of my savings.'

"'That's good. And what do you do with the coppers and silver you receive from the shield maker?'

"'I have a great feast with honey and fine drinks and cake. Also, I have bought a beautiful new robe. And someday soon I will buy a donkey to ride.' Farida laughed. 'You eat the fruit of your wealth tree. How do you expect them to bear you more fruit if you don't plant them? First, you have to get an army of coins and then, and only then, will you be able to buy whatever you want without regret.' After saying that, she again went away.

"I didn't see her for two years. When she finally returned, her face was full of deep lines and her eyes drooped. I could see she was becoming very old. And she said to me, 'Arkad, have you achieved the wealth you dreamed of?'

"And I answered, 'No, not all that I desire, not yet, but I have savings, and it earns more, and its earnings earn more.'

"'And do you still take the advice of brick makers?'

"'About brick making, they give very good advice,' I answered.

"'Arkad,'" she continued, 'you have learned your lessons well. You first learned to live on less than you earn. Next, you learned to seek advice from those who were competent through their own experiences to give it. And, lastly, you have learned to make your money work for you.

"'You have taught yourself how to acquire money, keep it, and use it. Therefore, I believe you are skilled and ready for a responsible position. I am becoming an old woman. My children only think of spending and give no thought to earning. My business is vast and I fear too big for me to continue to look after. If you go to Nippur and look after my lands there, I will make you my partner, and you will share in my business.'

"So I went to Nippur and looked after her business, which was indeed vast. And because I was full of ambition and had mastered the three laws of successfully handling wealth, I was able to significantly increase the value of her properties.

"So I prospered greatly, and when the spirit of Farida departed from this earth, I received part of her estate as she had agreed."

So concluded Arkad. And when he had finished his tale, one of his friends said, "You were indeed lucky that Farida made of you a partner."

"I was only fortunate that I had the desire to learn and prosper before I first met her. Didn't I prove myself by keeping one-tenth of all I earned for four years? Would you call someone who fishes lucky if they study the habits of the fish for years so that when the winds change, they could still cast their nets and bring in a profitable haul? Opportunity wastes no time on those who are unprepared."

"You had strong willpower to keep saving after you lost your first year's savings. You are unusual in that way," said another.

"Willpower?" retorted Arkad. "What nonsense. Do you think willpower gives a person the strength to lift a burden the camel can't carry or draw a load the oxen can't budge? Willpower is just the unflinching purpose to complete a task you set for yourself. If I set a task for myself, no matter how small, I will see it through. How else will I have confidence in myself to do important things? If I say to myself, 'For a hundred days as I walk across the bridge into the city, I will pick from the road a pebble and throw it into the stream,' I would do it. If on the seventh day I passed by without remembering, I wouldn't say to myself, tomorrow I will throw two pebbles which will be just as good. No, instead, I would retrace my steps and throw the pebble. Nor on the twentieth day would I say to myself, 'Arkad, this is useless. What is the point of throwing a pebble every day? Let me just throw in a handful and be done with it.' No, I wouldn't say that, nor do it. When I set a task for myself, I complete it. Therefore, I am careful not to start difficult and impractical tasks because I don't want to overburden myself and waste time that I could spend on more pleasant and enjoyable things."

And then another friend spoke up. "If your story is true, and it does seem reasonable, if everyone did it, there wouldn't be enough wealth to go around."

"Wealth grows wherever people exert energy," Arkad replied. "If someone with riches builds a new home, is the gold paid out gone? No, the brick maker has part of it, the builders have part of it, and the artist has part of it. And everyone who worked on the house has part of it. Yet when the house is completed, isn't it worth all it cost? And isn't the ground it stands on also worth more because the house is there? Wealth grows in magical ways. No one can predict the limit of it."

"OK, that was a nice story, but what should *we* do to become rich?" asked another one of his friends. "We are no longer young, and we've saved nothing."

"I would suggest that you use the wisdom of Farida as I did and say to yourselves, 'A part of all I earn is mine to keep.' Say it in the morning when you wake up. Say it at noon. Say it at night. Say it each hour of every day. Say it to yourself until the words stand out like letters written in fire across the sky.

"Convince yourself of the truth of the idea. Then take whatever amount seems wise. But never less than one-tenth, and set it aside. Arrange your other expenses to make this happen if necessary. But set aside that amount first. Soon you will realize what a rich feeling it is to own a treasure that you can call your own. As it grows, it will motivate you. A new joy of life will thrill you. More opportunities will come to you to earn more. And when your earnings increase, you will remember to set aside the same percentage, won't you?"

"Learn to make your savings work for you. Make your *savings* earn for you, and what your *earnings earn* work for you too.

"Ensure an income for your future. Remember, your working days are numbered. You won't be able to work forever. Therefore invest your savings with the greatest caution so that they won't be lost. Promises of great earnings on your savings are a warning sign, a signal for you to be extra careful, since those who promise a lot are often secretly offering you the opportunity to lose everything that you invest.

"Also, ensure your family is provided for and won't struggle when the Gods call you to their realms. To protect your family for that, take action now by making small regular payments to an insurer. The wise don't delay in preparing for the future.

"Consult with the wise. Seek the advice of those whose daily work is handling money. Let them save you from an error like I myself made in entrusting my money to the judgment of Azmur, the brick maker. A small and safe return is far more desirable than a risky gamble.

"Enjoy life while you are here. Don't burden yourself or try to save too much. If one-tenth of all you earn is as much as you can comfortably keep, be happy to save this amount. Otherwise, live according to your income and don't let yourself become greedy and afraid to spend. Life is good, and life is rich with things worthwhile and things to enjoy."

His friends thanked him and went away. Some were silent because they had no imagination and couldn't understand. Some were sarcastic because they thought someone as rich as Arkad should simply share what he had with old friends who weren't as fortunate. But some had a new light in their eyes. They realized that Farida had come back each time to the room of records because she was watching someone work their way out of the darkness into the light. When Arkad had found the light, a new reality appeared to him. No one could see that reality until they themselves understood the truth of Farida's teaching. Until then, they wouldn't be ready for the opportunity those truths revealed.

These friends, the ones who had seen the light in the following years, frequently revisited Arkad, who welcomed them gladly. He counseled them and freely gave them his wisdom, as people of broad experience are always happy to do. And he assisted them in how to invest their savings so that it would bring in a good return. As a result, they invested safely so their savings would neither be lost nor entangled in investments that paid no return.

The turning point in these friends' lives came that day when they realized the truth that had come from Farida to Arkad and from Arkad to them.

A PART OF ALL YOU EARN IS YOURS TO KEEP.

CHAPTER 3
SEVEN CURES FOR A
LEAN PURSE OR WALLET

T he glory of Babylon endures. Down through the ages, its
reputation comes to us as one of the wealthiest cities of all
time.

Yet, it wasn't always this way. The riches of Babylon were the
result of the wisdom of its people. They first had to learn how to
become wealthy.

When the Good King, Sargon, returned to Babylon after
defeating his enemies, he was confronted with a serious situation.
The king's counselor explained it to him.

"Your people have enjoyed years of great prosperity. Your
majesty's great irrigation canals and the mighty temples to the Gods
were huge successes, but unfortunately, now that these projects are
complete, the people seem unable to support themselves.

"The laborers have no work. The merchants have few customers.
The farmers are unable to sell their produce. The people don't have
enough gold to buy food."

"But where has all the gold gone that we spent on all of these
projects?" demanded the king.

"It has found its way, I fear," responded the counselor, "into the hands of the few very rich of our city. It slips through the fingers of most of our people as quickly as water goes through cloth. Now that our city projects are completed, the stream of gold has stopped flowing, and most of our people have nothing to earn."

The king was thoughtful for some time. Then he asked, "Why should so few be able to acquire all the gold?"

"Because they know how," replied the counselor. "We shouldn't criticize someone for succeeding because they know how obtain wealth. Nor would it be just to take away the riches from someone who has earned them fairly, to give to someone of less ability."

"But why," demanded the king, "shouldn't all the people learn how to accumulate gold and become rich and prosperous?"

"I suppose that's possible, your excellency. But who can teach them? Certainly not the priests because they don't know how to gain wealth."

"Then who knows best how to become wealthy in our city, counselor?" asked the king.

"Your question answers itself, your majesty. Who has amassed the greatest wealth in Babylon?"

"Well said, counselor. It's Arkad. He is the richest person in Babylon. Bring him to me tomorrow."

As the king had ordered, Arkad appeared before him the following day, straight and alert despite his seventy years.

"Arkad, is it true you are the richest person in Babylon?" asked the king.

"Yes, your majesty, and as far as I am aware, no one disagrees."

"How did you become so wealthy?"

"By taking advantage of opportunities available to all citizens of our good city."

"You weren't born rich? You started with nothing?"

"Only a great desire for wealth. Besides that, nothing."

"Arkad," continued the king, "our city is in a miserable state because only a few know how to acquire wealth and therefore monopolize it, while the majority of our citizens lack the knowledge of how to keep any part of the gold they receive.

"I want Babylon to be the wealthiest city in the world. Therefore, it must be a city of many wealthy citizens. We must teach all the people how to acquire riches. Tell me, Arkad, is there any secret to acquiring wealth? Can it be taught?"

"It's possible, your majesty. Something that one knows can be taught to others."

The king's eyes glowed. "Arkad, you speak the words I want to hear. Will you lend yourself to this great cause? Will you teach your knowledge to a school for teachers, each of whom will teach others until there are enough trained to teach these truths to every worthy subject in my kingdom?"

Arkad bowed and said, "I am your humble servant to command. Whatever knowledge I possess I will gladly give for the betterment of my neighbors and the glory of my king. Let your good counselor arrange a class of one hundred people, and I will teach them the seven cures that fill my wallet, a wallet that used to be the emptiest in all of Babylon."

Two weeks later, as the king had commanded, the chosen hundred assembled in the great hall of the Temple of Learning, seated on colorful rugs in a semicircle. Arkad sat beside a small table on which a lit candle sent up plumes of a strange and pleasing smoke.

"Behold the richest person in Babylon," whispered a student, nudging their neighbor as Arkad arose. "He is just a person just like the rest of us."

"As an obedient subject of our great king," Arkad began, "I stand before you in his service. Because once I was a poor youth who greatly desired gold, and because I found knowledge that enabled me to acquire it, he has asked that I impart my knowledge to you.

"I started my fortune in the humblest way. I had no advantage. There was nothing special I held that was not available to every citizen in Babylon.

"The first warehouse of my treasure was a full wallet. As a youth, I hated its useless emptiness. I wanted my wallet to be round and full, clinking with the sound of gold. So I searched every solution for a light wallet. I found seven.

"To you who are assembled before me, I will explain the seven solutions for a light wallet that I recommend to all who desire a lot of gold. Each day for seven days, I will present one of the seven solutions.

"Listen closely to the knowledge that I will give to you. Debate it with me. Discuss it among yourselves. Learn these lessons thoroughly so that you may also plant in your own wallet or purse the seed of wealth. But, first, each of you must start to build a fortune of your own. Only then will you be able to teach these truths to others.

"I will teach to you in simple ways how to fatten your wallets and purses. This is your first step leading to the temple of wealth, and no one may climb who can't plant their feet firmly on the first step.

"We will now consider the first solution."

THE FIRST CURE ~ START FATTENING YOUR WALLETS AND PURSES

Arkad addressed a thoughtful student in the second row. "My good friend, what craft do you practice?"

"I," replied the student, "am a record-keeper and carve records on clay tablets."

"That was the very thing I did to earn my first coppers. Therefore, you have the same opportunity as I did to build a fortune."

He spoke to a rosy-cheeked student farther back. "Please, tell us what you do to earn a living?"

"I am a butcher," responded the student. "I buy the goats the farmers raise and kill them and sell the meat in the market and the hides to the sandal makers."

"Because you also work and earn, you too also have everything you need to succeed that I did."

In this manner, Arkad proceeded to find out how each student worked to earn their living. Then, when he was done questioning them, he said:

"Now, my students, you can see that there are many ways that you can earn money. Each way of earning creates a stream of gold from your work into your wallets or purses. Since each of you works, you all have a flow of income. How much you earn will then depend on your skills and ability. Is that not right?"

The students agreed that was, in fact, true. "Then," continued Arkad, "if each of you wants to build a fortune for yourselves, wouldn't it be wise to start by using that source of wealth which you have already established?"

They agreed with this as well.

Then Arkad turned to a humble student who had identified themself as an egg merchant. "If you select one of your baskets and put into it each morning ten eggs and take out from it each evening nine eggs, what will eventually happen?"

"It will, over time, start to overflow."

"Why?"

"Because each day, I put in one more egg than I take out."

Arkad turned to the class with a smile. "Does anyone here have an empty wallet or purse?"

First, they looked amused. Then they laughed. Lastly, they waved their wallets and purses in the air as a joke.

"All right," he continued, "now I will tell you the first solution I learned to fix my empty wallet. Do exactly as I have suggested to the egg merchant. For every ten coins you place in your wallet or purse, take out for use only nine. Your wallets and purses will start to fatten at once, and their increasing weight will feel good in your hands and bring satisfaction to your soul.

"Don't mock what I say because of its simplicity. Truth is always simple. I told you I would describe how I built my fortune. This was my beginning. I also carried an empty wallet and cursed it because nothing was there to satisfy my desires. But when I began to take out from my wallet only nine parts of the ten I put in, it began to fatten. So will yours.

"Now, I will tell a strange truth. Why it's true, I don't know. When I stopped paying out more than nine-tenths of my earnings, I managed to get along just fine. I wasn't poorer than before. Also, before long, coins came to me more easily than before. Surely it's a law of the Gods that for those who keep and spend only a certain part of their earnings, gold will come more easily. Similarly, it seems like gold avoids those whose wallets are always empty.

"What do you desire the most? Is it the gratification of your daily wishes, a bit of jewelry, a new outfit, fine food? These things are gone quickly, but if you wish for them, take the gold when you receive it and buy them. But if you desire more gold, property, and wealth, you must leave some coins in your wallet or purse. The coins in your wallet and purse will earn you more money tomorrow.

"This, my students, was the first solution I discovered for my empty wallet: for every ten coins I put in, I spend only nine. Debate this amongst yourselves. If anyone proves it wrong, tell me tomorrow when we meet again."

～

THE SECOND CURE ~ CONTROL YOUR EXPENSES

"Some of you, my students, have asked me this: how can we keep one-tenth of all we earn in our wallets and purses when all the coins we earn aren't enough for our necessities?" This is how Arkad addressed his students on the second day.

"Yesterday how many of you carried empty wallets and purses?"

"All of us," answered the class.

"Yet, you don't all earn the same amount. Some earn much more than others. Some have much larger families to support. Yet, all of your wallets and purses were empty. Now I will tell you an unusual truth about people . What each of us calls our *necessary expenses* will always grow equal to our incomes unless we intentionally strive to ensure it doesn't.

"Don't confuse necessary expenses with your desires. Each of you, together with your good families, have more desires than your earnings can possibly satisfy. Therefore your earnings are spent to satisfy these desires as much as they can. But even if you spent every copper you earned, you would still have many unsatisfied desires.

"All people are burdened with more desires than they can satisfy. Do you think that because of my wealth I may satisfy every desire? Of course not. There are limits to my time. There are limits to my strength, the distance I may travel, or to how much I can eat.

"Just as weeds grow in a field wherever the farmer leaves space for their roots, so too do desires grow in people whenever there is a possibility they may be satisfied. Your desires are large in number and those that you may satisfy are few.

"Look carefully at your living habits. This is where you will most often find certain expenses that it may be wise to reduce or elimi-nate. You should seek, or rather *demand*, the most value for each coin spent.

"Write down each thing that you want to spend on. Select the items that are truly necessary and others that are still possible to have when using only nine-tenths of your income. Cross out the rest and consider them to be a part of that great number of desires that must go unsatisfied, and don't trouble yourself with them.

"Budget for your necessary expenses. Don't touch the one-tenth that's fattening your wallet or purse. Make your fattening wallet and purses be the one desire that's fulfilled before any other. Keep working with your budget; keep adjusting it to help you. Make it guard to help you defend your growing wealth."

At this point one of the students, wearing a robe of red and gold, stood and said, "I am a free person. I believe that it's my right to enjoy the good things of life. I am against being under the rule of a budget which determines just how much I may spend and for what. I feel it would take much of the pleasure from my life and make me little more than a workhorse carrying a heavy load."

To the student Arkad replied, "Who, my friend, would determine your budget?"

"I would make it for myself," responded the protesting student.

"In that case may I ask if a workhorse were to budget its load would it include jewels and rugs and heavy bars of gold as its cargo? Of course not. It would include hay and grain and a bag of water for the desert trail.

"The purpose of a budget is to help you fatten your wallet. It's to help you get the necessities and as much as you can afford of your other desires. It's to enable you to obtain the things you desire above everything else by defending them from your casual wishes. Like a bright light in a dark cave, your budget shows the leaks from your wallets and purses and enables you to stop them and control your expenses.

"This, then, is the second solution for an empty wallet or purse. Budget your expenses so that you will have coins to pay for your necessities, for your enjoyment, and to satisfy your worthwhile desires without spending more than nine-tenths of your earnings."

～

THE THIRD CURE ~ MAKE YOUR GOLD MULTIPLY

"Your empty wallets and purses are now on their way to fattening. You have disciplined yourself to set aside one-tenth of all you earn. You have controlled your expenses to protect your growing fortunes. Next, we will consider how to put your treasure to work to increase it. Gold in a wallet or purse is satisfying to own and satisfies a hoarder's soul, but earns nothing. The gold we keep from our earnings is just the start. The earnings it will make is what will build our fortunes." This is what Arkad said on the third day to his class.

"How should we put our gold to work? My first investment was unfortunate because I lost it all. It's a tale I will tell later. But my first profitable investment was a loan I made to a shield maker named Aaliyah. Once each year, Aaliyah would buy large shipments of bronze brought from across the sea to use in shield making. Lacking enough gold to pay the merchants, Aaliyah would borrow from those who had extra coins. She was known for being honorable. She would repay what she borrowed along with a reasonable interest payment as she sold her shields.

"Each time I loaned to Aaliyah, I also lent her the interest earnings from my past loans as part of the new loan. So not only did my initial investment increase but what I was earning also increased. It was incredibly gratifying to see my investment grow and grow.

"I tell you, my students, your wealth isn't in the coins you carry in your wallets and purses; it's the income you build, the streams of coins that continually flow into your wallets and purses and keep them always fat. That's what everyone desires. That's what each one of you wants: an income that continues to come in whether you work or travel.

"I have acquired great wealth. So great that I am called the richest person in Babylon. My loans to Aaliyah were my first training in profitable investment. Gaining wisdom from this experience, I extended my loans and investments as my wealth increased. From a few sources at first to many later. Each source flowed into my wallet a stream of wealth available, to use for whatever I might desire.

"You can see, from my humble earnings, I had created an army of golden employees, each working and earning more gold. As they worked for me, so too will their offspring also work, and their offspring's offspring, until my income was great from their combined efforts.

"Gold increases rapidly when making reasonable earnings, as you will see from this example. When his first child was born, a farmer took ten pieces of silver to a moneylender and asked the lender to keep it as an investment for his child until the child became twenty years old. The moneylender did what was asked and agreed that they would pay the amount of one-fourth of its value every four years. In addition, the farmer asked that all interest earned be added to the original investment to be reinvested.

"When the child reached twenty years old, the farmer went to the moneylender to ask about the silver. The moneylender explained that because the interest earned on the investment was reinvested, the original ten pieces of silver had now grown to thirty and a half pieces. The moneylender called this growth compound interest.

"The farmer was pleased, and because the child didn't need the coins, the farmer left them with the moneylender. When the child became fifty years old, and the farmer in the meantime had passed to the other world, the moneylender paid the child one hundred and sixty-seven pieces of silver.

"This is why after fifty years, the investment of ten silver coins was able to increase itself by almost seventeen times.

So this is the third solution for an empty wallet and purse: put each coin saved to work so that it may reproduce itself even as you sleep, helping to bring you an income stream of wealth that will constantly flow into your wallets and purses."

～

THE FOURTH CURE ~ GUARD YOUR SAVINGS AGAINST LOSS

"Misfortune loves an easy target. That's why gold in one's wallet or purse must be guarded with determination, or it will be lost. This is why we must first learn to secure small amounts and protect them before the Gods entrust us with larger sums." This is what Arkad said on the fourth day to the class.

"Every owner of gold is tempted by opportunities where it would seem that they could make large returns by some investment. Often friends and relatives are entering into these types of investments and will urge you to follow.

"The first sound rule of investment is securing your investment. Is it wise to be tempted by large returns when you might lose your initial investment? I say no. The penalty for your bad judgment is a loss of your investment. Carefully study your opportunity before investing. Seek out a guarantee that your investment will be safely returned where possible. Don't let your desire to become wealthy quickly lead you down a path you can't return from.

"Before you loan anything to anyone, assure yourself of the borrower's ability to repay and their reputation for repaying so that you may not mistakenly be gifting them a present of your hard-earned savings.

"Before you invest in any field, take time to learn the risks that come with that investment opportunity.

"My own first investment was a tragedy to me at the time. I entrusted the savings I had accumulated and guarded for a year to a brick maker named Azmur, who was travelling over the far seas and in Tyre agreed to buy the rare jewels of the Phoenicians for me. We planned to sell these when Azmur returned and divide the profits. Unfortunately, the Phoenicians were cheats and sold him bits of glass. My savings were lost. Today, my training would show to me at once the mistake of trusting a brick maker to buy jewels.

"Therefore, I advise you from the wisdom of my experience: don't become too confident in your own knowledge when investing. It's much better to consult those experienced in handling money for profit. Such advice is often given freely and may have a value equal in gold to what you may be investing. The value of your savings is the value of the advice you receive from wise advisors if what they give you saves you from loss.

"This, then, is the fourth solution for a light purse or wallet and is of great importance if it prevents your purse or wallet from being emptied once it has become full. Guard your savings against loss by investing only where your initial investment will be safe, where it may be reclaimed if you want it back, and where you won't fail to collect a fair return. Consult with the wise. Secure the advice of those experienced in the profitable handling of gold. Let their wisdom protect your treasure from unsafe investments."

~

THE FIFTH CURE ~ MAKE YOUR HOME A PROFITABLE INVESTMENT

"If you work and set aside nine parts of your earnings to live on and enjoy life, and if any part of those nine parts can be turned into a profitable investment without hurting your well-being, then wouldn't your wealth grow faster?" Arkad asked his class this at their fifth lesson.

"All too many of our citizens of Babylon raise their families in unsuitable homes. They pay unkind landlords too much rent for rooms where their families don't have proper space to rest and relax, and their children have no place to play their games except in the dirty alleys.

"No one's family can fully enjoy life unless they have a plot of land where children can play in the clean earth and where they may plant a small garden with vegetables and herbs to feed their family.

"Your heart would be warmed if you could eat the figs from your own trees and the grapes off your own vines. To own a home and have it be a place to be proud of and care for puts confidence in your heart and conviction behind all your endeavors. So, I recommend that every family should work to own the roof that shelters it.

"I don't think that it's beyond the ability of any well-intentioned person to own their home. Hasn't our great king extended the walls of Babylon so that there is much-unused land that may be purchased at a reasonable amount within them?

"Also, my students, moneylenders gladly consider the desires of those who seek homes and land for their families. You may easily borrow to pay the brick maker and the builder for such noble purposes if you can show you have saved a reasonable portion of the required sum – what they call a deposit.

"Then, when the house is built, you can pay the moneylender with the same regularity as you once paid the landlord, and because each payment will reduce your debt to the moneylender, after a few years, you will have paid off the loan.

"Then your heart be will be pleased because you will own your own valuable property, and your only cost will be the king's taxes.

"Many blessings come to the one who owns their own home. It will greatly reduce your cost of living, making more of your earnings available for pleasures and the gratification of your desires. This, then, is the fifth cure for a lean purse or wallet: own your own home."

THE SIXTH CURE ~ ENSURE A FUTURE INCOME

"The life of every person born proceeds from their childhood to old age. This is the path of life, and no one may deviate from it unless the Gods call them prematurely to the world beyond. Therefore, listen to these words. It's in everyone's best interest to prepare for a suitable income in the days to come, when you are no longer young, and make preparations for your family in case you are no longer with them to comfort and support them. This lesson will instruct you in providing a full purse or wallet when time and old age make you less able to earn." So Arkad addressed his class on the sixth day.

"The one who, because of their understanding of the laws of wealth, acquires a growing savings, should give thought to the future. They should plan certain investments or provisions that may endure safely for many years, yet will be available when the time arrives, which they have so wisely anticipated.

"There are many ways in which a person may provide for their future with safety. They may provide a hiding place to bury a secret treasure, but no matter how much skill is used to hide it, it may still become the booty of thieves. For this reason, I don't recommend this plan.

"You may buy houses or lands for this purpose. If wisely chosen they may increase and retain their value for years. Their sale may provide well for this purpose.

"You may loan a small sum to the moneylender and contribute payments at regular intervals. Naturally, the interest which the moneylender adds to this will increase its total. I do know a sandal maker named Ansan, who explained to me not long ago that each week for eight years, they had deposited with their moneylender two pieces of silver. The moneylender had recently given them the balance of the investment, for which they were overjoyed. The total of the small deposits and the interest earned at the standard rate of one-fourth their value for every four years had now become a thousand and forty pieces of silver.

"I encouraged them further by using my skills with numbers that in twelve more years if they would keep this deposit schedule of two pieces of silver each week, the moneylender would then owe Ansan four thousand pieces of silver. A tidy sum that could be used for the rest of their life.

"Surely, when such a small payment made consistently can produce such profitable results, no one can afford *not* to ensure a savings for their old age and the protection of their family, no matter how prosperous their business and investments may be.

"But there is more that I would like to say about this. I foresee a day when wise-thinking people will devise a plan to ensure against death. Many people will pay a tiny sum regularly, and the total of these many small payments by many people would make a handsome sum for the family of each member who passes to the beyond. This I see as something desirable and which I would highly recommend.

"But today, it's not possible because it must reach beyond any one person's life or any partnership to operate. It must be as stable as the king's throne. But someday, I feel that such a plan will come to pass and be a great blessing to everyone because even the first small payment will make available a comfortable fortune for the family of a member who passes on.

"But because we live in our day and not in the days which are to come, we have to take advantage of the means and ways of the current day in order to accomplish our purposes. So, I recommend that everyone provide against a lean purse or wallet in their mature years by well-thought-out methods. A lean purse or wallet to a person who can no longer earn is a challenge you need to avoid. A family without the means to earn an income is a great tragedy. This, then, is the sixth cure for a lean purse or wallet. Provide in advance for the needs of your growing age and the protection of your family."

∾

THE SEVENTH CURE ~ INCREASE YOUR ABILITY TO EARN

"Today, my students, I will speak with you about one of the most vital remedies for a lean purse or wallet. Yet, I won't talk about gold but of yourselves, of the students who sit before me. I will talk to you about those things within the minds and lives of people which will work for or against their success." This is how Arkad addressed his class on the seventh day.

"Not long ago, a young woman came to me seeking a loan. When I questioned her need for the loan, she complained that her earnings were insufficient to pay her expenses. I then explained to her that this being the case, she was a poor customer for the moneylender, as she had no extra earning capacity to repay the loan.

'Why do you, young lady, need a loan?' I asked her 'Is it to earn more coins? What have you done to increase your ability to earn?'

"'All that I can do,' she replied. 'Six times within two months I have approached my employer to request my pay be increased, but without success. No one can go more often than that.'

"We may smile at her simplicity, yet she did possess one of the vital requirements to increase her earnings. A strong desire, genuine and commendable, to earn more was within her.

"Before accomplishment must be desire. Your desires must be strong and defined. General desires or goals are just weak wishes. For someone to want to be rich serves little purpose. For someone to desire five pieces of gold is a tangible desire that they can work to fulfill. After they have worked with strength of purpose in obtaining the five pieces of gold, they can find similar ways to obtain ten pieces, and then twenty pieces, and later a thousand pieces and, behold, they will have become wealthy. In learning to secure their one defined small desire, they have trained themself to secure a larger one. This is how wealth is accumulated: first in small sums, then in larger ones as a person learns and becomes more capable.

Desires must be simple and defined. They defeat their own

purpose if there are too many, too confusing, or beyond a person's training to accomplish.

"As we perfect ourselves in our vocation, so too does our ability to earn increase. In those days when I was a humble record-keeper carving on clay for a few coppers each day, I observed that other workers did more than I did and were paid more. Therefore, I determined that I would need to be one of the best to earn the most I could. It didn't take long for me to discover the reason for my co-workers' success. I took more interest in my work, concentrated more on my tasks, and dedicated more persistence in my effort, and before long few could carve more tablets in a day than I could. Within a reasonable time, my increased skills were recognized and rewarded, all without having to go to my employer once to ask for a wage increase, let alone six times in two months.

"The more knowledge and skills we gain, the more we can earn. Therefore, the person who tries to learn more about their craft will be richly rewarded. If they are an artisan, they may try to learn the methods and tools of those most skillful people in the same trade. If they work in law or medicine, they may consult and exchange knowledge with others in those careers. If they are a merchant, they may continually seek better goods that can be purchased at lower prices.

"Keen-minded people who are always improving their skills to serve their clients better will do well. They cater to our desires to get the best at the best prices. So I urge you all to take the lead and innovate and adopt new technologies and strategies when you can or you'll be left behind.

"Many things will happen to make a person's life rich with useful experiences. A person has to do things like the following if they want to respect themself:

"They must pay their debts as promptly as they can, and not purchase things that are beyond their ability to pay for.

"They must take care of their family so that the family members think highly of them and talk about them positively.

"They must make a will of record so that in case the Gods call them, a proper and honorable division of their property can be made.

"They must have compassion for those who are injured and unfortunate, and help them within reasonable limits. They must do thoughtful and kind things for those who are dear to them.

"Thus, the seventh and last remedy for a lean purse or wallet is to cultivate your own powers, study and become wiser, become more skillful, and respect yourself in the actions you take towards others. That's how you will acquire confidence in yourself to achieve your carefully thought-out dreams.

"These then are the seven cures for a lean purse or wallet, which, out of my experience of a long and successful life, I urge for everyone who desires wealth. There is more gold in Babylon, my students, than you can even dream of. There is lots for everyone.

"Go and practice these truths so that you can prosper and grow wealthy, which you are entitled to.

"Go out and teach these truths so that every honorable subject of Babylon can also share liberally in the abundant wealth of our beloved city."

CHAPTER 4
HOW TO ATTRACT GOOD LUCK

" If a person is lucky, there is no foretelling the possible extent of their good fortune. Pitch them into the Euphrates and they'll likely swim out with a pearl in their hand." – Babylonian Proverb

The desire to be lucky is universal. It was just as strong in the heart of the people in ancient Babylon four thousand years ago as it is in the hearts of people today. We all hope to be favored by the whimsical God of Good Luck.

Is there some way we can meet luck and attract not only its favorable attention but its generous favors? Is there a way to attract good luck?

That's just what the citizens of ancient Babylon wanted to know. It's what they decided to find out. They were wise and keen thinkers. That explains why their city became the richest and most powerful city of their time.

In that distant past, they had no schools or colleges. Nevertheless, they had an efficient center of learning. Among the towering buildings in Babylon, one was ranked at the same level of importance as the Palace of the king, the Hanging Gardens, and the Gods' temples. You will find little mention of it in the history books, if any mention at all, yet it exerted a powerful influence on the thought of the time.

This building was the Temple of Learning, where voluntary teachers presented the wisdom of the past, and where subjects of popular interest were discussed in open forums. Within its walls, everyone met as equals. The humblest person could debate without fear of the opinions of a member of the royal house.

Among the many who frequented the Temple of Learning was a wise rich citizen named Arkad, who was called the richest person in all of Babylon. He had his own special hall where almost any evening a large group of students, some old, some very young, but mostly middle-aged, gathered to discuss and debate interesting subjects. Let's listen in to see whether they knew how to attract good luck.

The sun had just set like a great red ball of fire shining through the haze of desert dust when Arkad strolled to his accustomed platform. Already eighty students were awaiting his arrival, reclining on their small rugs spread on the floor. More were still arriving.

"What will we discuss tonight?" Arkad asked.

After a brief hesitation, a tall cloth weaver addressed him, standing, as was the custom. "I have a subject I would like to hear discussed yet hesitate to offer for fear that it may seem ridiculous to you, Arkad, and my good friends here."

On being urged to offer it by both Arkad and by pleas from the others, the student continued: "Today I have been lucky, because I have found a bag in which there are pieces of gold. My great desire is to continue to be lucky. Feeling that you all share this desire, I suggest we debate how to attract good luck."

"A most interesting subject," Arkad commented, "one worthy of our discussion. To some, good luck suggests a chance happening that, like an accident, may happen without purpose or reason. Others believe that the cause of all good fortune comes from the Gods, who are always ready to reward those who please them with generous gifts. So speak up, my friends, what do you say, should we try to find if there is a way to invite good luck to visit each of us?"

"Yea! Yea! And much of it!" responded the growing group of eager listeners.

So Arkad continued. "To start our discussion, let's first hear from those among us who have enjoyed experiences similar to that of the cloth weaver in finding or receiving, without effort on their part, valuable treasures or jewels."

There was a pause during which all looked around, expecting someone to reply, but no one did.

"What, no one?" Arkad said. "Then it's rare indeed, this kind of good luck. Who now will offer a suggestion as to where we will continue our search for good luck?"

"I will," spoke a well-dressed young student, standing up. "When we speak of luck, isn't it natural that our thoughts turn to gambling at the gaming tables? Isn't it there we find many seeking the favor of the Gods of Luck, hoping they will bless them with rich winnings?"

As the student sat down, a voice shouted, "Don't stop! Continue your story! Tell us, did you find luck at the gaming tables? Did the cubes land with the red side up for you to fill your pockets, or did the Gods let the blue sides come up so the dealer would take in your hard-earned pieces of silver?"

The young student joined the good-natured laughter, then replied, "To tell you the truth, I don't think the God of Luck even knew I was there. But how about the rest of you? Have you found luck's favor waiting for you in places of chance? We are eager to hear as well as to learn."

"A wise start," Arkad interrupted. "We are meeting here to consider all sides of each question. Ignoring the gaming table would be overlooking a desire common to many people, the love of taking a chance with a small amount of silver in the hope of winning much gold."

"That reminds me of the races yesterday," said another listener.

"If the God of Luck visits the gaming tables, certainly it would look down on the races where the golden chariots and the panting horses offer far more excitement. Tell us honestly, Arkad, did the God whisper to you to place your bet on that gray horse from Nineveh yesterday? I was standing just behind you and could hardly believe my ears when I heard you place your bet. Especially since you know as well as any of us that horses from Assyria can beat ours in a fair race.

"Did the Gods whisper in your ear to bet on the gray horse because they knew that the black horse would stumble into our town's horse, causing it to lose the lead, and that the gray horse would win the race with an unearned victory?"

Arkad smiled unworriedly at the discussion. "Do we have any reason to believe that any God would take an interest in anyone's bet in a horse race? To me, the God of Luck is more concerned about love and dignity and would rather help those in need and reward the deserving. So I look to luck, not at the gaming tables or the races where players lose more gold than they win, but in other places where our actions are more worthwhile and worthy of reward.

"In all of our work, there is an opportunity to make a profit on our efforts and transactions. Perhaps we won't always be rewarded, because sometimes our judgment may be faulty, and other times the winds and the weather may defeat our efforts. Yet, if we persist, we can usually expect to realize a profit. This is because the chances of profit are always in our favor.

"But, when we play games the situation is reversed. The chances of profit are always against us and always in favor of the game-keeper. The game is arranged so that it will always favor the keeper. It's the gamekeeper's business at which they plan to make a great profit for themselves from the coins bet by the players. Few players realize how guaranteed the gamekeeper's profits are and how unlikely their chances to win are.

"For example, let's consider bets placed on the cube. Each time it's thrown, we bet which side will land up. If it's the red side, the gamemaster pays us four times our bet. But if any other of the five sides come up, we lose our bet. If we think it through, we can see that we have five chances to lose for each throw, but we have four chances to win because the red pays four for one. In a night's play, the gamemaster can expect to keep one-fifth of all the coins that were gambled for his profit. Can anyone expect to win more than a little bit and only occasionally when the odds are created for them to lose one-fifth of all of their bets?"

"Yet some people do win large amounts at times," volunteered one of the listeners.

"Quite right, they do," Arkad continued. "Realizing this, the question comes to me whether money secured in such ways brings permanent value to those who are so lucky. Among my acquaintances are many of the successful people of Babylon, yet among them, I am unable to name a single one who started their success from such a source.

"You who are gathered here tonight know many of our wealthy citizens. It would be very interesting to learn if any successful citizens can attribute their successful beginning to the gaming tables. Tell me about anyone you know who got their start to success at the gaming tables?"

After a long silence, someone ventured, "Could we not include the gamekeepers themselves?"

"If you can think of no one else," Arkad responded.

"If not one of you can think of anyone else, then how about yourselves? Are there any consistent winners with us who advise the gaming tables as a source for their incomes?"

Arkad's challenge was answered by laughter and a series of groans from the back.

"It would seem we aren't looking for good luck in places we hoped to find it," he continued. "We haven't found it in picking up lost wallets. And we haven't found it around the gaming tables. As for the horse races, I must confess to having lost far more coins there than I have ever won.

"Now, suppose we consider our businesses. Let's say we were to complete a business deal that worked out in our favor. Would we call this luck or just the reward for our hard work? I believe most of you here would agree we don't think about the God of Luck at all in this scenario. But maybe it was luck, and we just didn't realize it or appreciate its generosity. So what do you all think of this?"

At that point, an elderly merchant stood up, smoothing her white robe. "With your permission, most honorable Arkad and my friends, I offer a suggestion. If it's as you have said, and we take credit for our hard work and ability when our business is successful, why don't we consider the successes we almost enjoyed but that escaped us for one reason or another. Those would be examples of good luck if they had actually happened. But because they weren't successful, we can't consider them as our rewards for our hard work. Surely many here have experiences like this they can relate to."

"This is a wise approach," Arkad approved. "Who here has had good luck within your reach, only to see it slip away?"

Many hands were raised, including the white-robed merchant. Arkad motioned to her to speak. "As you suggested this approach, we would like to hear from you first."

"I will gladly tell my story," she resumed, "a story that shows how closely good luck may approach, and how quickly it can escape, much to my loss and later regret.

"Many years ago, when I was young and just married, my parents came to me one day and strongly urged me to make an investment. A friend of theirs had noticed an empty piece of land not too far beyond the outer city walls. It was high above the canal where no water could reach it.

"The friend had worked out a plan to purchase this land, build three large water wheels that could be operated by oxen, and raise the waters to the fertile soil. Once this was accomplished, they planned to divide the land into small lots and sell them to the city's residents for agriculture.

"My parents' friend didn't have enough gold to complete this project. Like myself, they were young, working, and making enough money. Their parents, like mine, had grown up in large families with little means. This friend, therefore, decided to create a group of interested people to enter into the business. The group was comprised of twelve people, each of whom had to be a money earner and agree to pay one-tenth of their earnings into the enterprise until the land was ready for sale. All group members would then share in the profits equal to the proportion of their investment.

"My parents encouraged me by saying, 'You are young, and it's our deep desire that you begin the building of a valuable estate for yourself so that you become respected among the citizens of this city. We want to see you profit from and learn from the thoughtless mistakes of your parents.'

"'I hope to grow wealthy and make you both proud,' I replied.

"'Then follow this advice. Do what we should have done at your age. From your earnings, take out one-tenth to put into sound investments. With this one-tenth of your earnings and what it will also earn, you can, before you are our age, accumulate a valuable estate for yourself.'

"'You are both wise. I really want to be rich. Yet there are so many things I need to use my earnings for. While I trust you, I do hesitate to do as you say. I am young. There is plenty of time to earn a fortune.'

"'That's what we said at your age, yet look, many years have passed, and we've not even started to save.'

"'We live in a different time. I will avoid your mistakes.'

"'Opportunity stands before you, my child. It's offering you a chance that may lead to wealth. I beg you, don't delay. Go tomorrow to this friend and bargain with them to pay ten percent of your earnings into this investment. Go right away. Opportunity waits for no one. Today it's here; soon, it's gone. Don't delay!'

"Despite the advice of my parents, I did hesitate. There were beautiful new robes just brought by traders from the East, robes of such richness and beauty my partner and I both felt we had to have one. If I agreed to pay one-tenth of my earnings into the enterprise, we would have to deprive ourselves of these and other pleasures we strongly desired. I delayed making a decision until it was too late, much to my regret. Nevertheless, the enterprise did turn out to be more profitable than anyone had guessed. This is my tale, showing how I let good luck escape me."

"In this tale, we see how good luck waits to come to those who accept an opportunity," commented a dusty herder of the desert. "To start the building of wealth, there must always be a beginning. That start may be a few pieces of gold or silver which you divert from your earnings into your first investment. I myself am the owner of many herds. My wealth began when I was a mere child, and I purchased a young calf with one piece of silver. This was the beginning of my wealth and was of great importance to me.

"To take steps to start building an estate is the best luck that can come to anyone. With all people, that first step, which changes them from those who earn from their labor to those who draw dividends from the earnings of their gold, is important. Some, fortunately, take it when they're young and by doing so leave behind those who take it later, or those unfortunate few, like the parents of this merchant, who never take it.

"If our friend, the merchant, had taken this step in her early days when this opportunity came to her, by now she would have amassed a tidy fortune. If the good luck of our friend, the cloth weaver, causes them to take such a step at this time, it would indeed be just the beginning of much greater good fortune."

"Thank you! I would like to speak, also." A stranger from another country arose. "I don't speak your language well. I want to call this friend, the merchant, a name. Maybe you don't think it's polite, this name. Yet I want to call her that. But, alas, I don't know your word for it. If I do say it in my language, you won't understand. Therefore, please, good friends, tell me that right name you call a person who puts off doing those things that might be good for them."

"Procrastinator," called a voice.

"That's it," shouted the stranger, waving their hands excitedly. "She didn't accept opportunity when it came. She waits. She says I have too much to do right now. I will do it later. Opportunity won't wait for someone so slow to act. Opportunity thinks that if you want to be lucky, you will act quickly. Anyone who doesn't act quickly when an opportunity comes is a big procrastinator like our friend, this merchant."

The merchant stood and bowed good-naturedly in response to the laughter. "Thank you to this stranger who doesn't hesitate to speak the truth."

"And now let's hear another tale of opportunity. Who has another experience for us?" requested Arkad.

"I do," responded a red-robed man of middle age. "I am a buyer of animals, mostly camels and horses. Sometimes I do also buy sheep and goats. The tale I am about to tell will show how an opportunity came one night when I least expected it. Maybe that was the reason I let it escape. You be the judge.

"Returning to the city one evening after a dismal ten-day journey in search of camels, I was angry to find the gates of the city closed and locked. I was even more upset by the locked gates since we had little food and no water for the long night ahead. While my staff spread our tent for the night, I was approached by an elderly farmer. This farmer, like ourselves, was locked outside.

"'Honored sir,' I was addressed, 'would I be mistaken in assuming that you are a buyer of livestock. If I am correct, I would very much like to sell you the most excellent flock of sheep. Unfortunately, my child is very sick with a fever. I must return home with all haste. Please buy my sheep so that I may travel back without delay.'

"It was so dark that I couldn't see his flock, but from the bleating, I knew it must be enormous. Having wasted ten days searching for camels I couldn't find, I was glad to bargain with him. In his anxiety, he set a very reasonable price. I accepted, knowing my staff could move the flock through the city gates in the morning and sell them at a substantial profit.

"With the deal concluded, I called my staff to bring torches to count the flock, which the farmer claimed to contain nine hundred. I won't burden you, my friends, with a description of our difficulty in trying to count so many thirsty, restless sheep. It proved to be an impossible task. Therefore, I bluntly told the farmer I would count them the next day and pay him then.

"'Please, most honorable sir,' the farmer pleaded, 'pay me only two-thirds of the price tonight so that I can be on my way. I will leave my most intelligent and educated staff to help you with the count in the morning. They are trustworthy, and you can pay them what you owe me.'

"But I was stubborn and refused to make a payment that night. The next morning, before I awoke, the city gates opened, and four buyers rushed out in search of flocks. They were very eager and willing to pay high prices because of the shortages in the city. The farmer received nearly three times the price he had offered the flock to me. That was how I allowed rare good luck to escape."

"Here is a tale most unusual," commented Arkad. "What wisdom does it suggest?"

"The wisdom of making a payment immediately when we are convinced our bargain is wise," suggested a well-respected saddle maker. "If the bargain is good, then you may need protection against your indecisiveness, just as much as you may need protection from a cheater or a thief. We mortals are inconsistent. Unfortunately, I find we are more prone to change our minds when we are right than wrong. When we are wrong, we are stubborn and dig our heels in. When we are right, we often flip-flop and let opportunities escape. My first decision is often my best. Yet I have always found it difficult to proceed with a good bargain when it's made. To protect against wavering, I make a prompt deposit to secure my position. This saves me from later regrets for the good luck that should have been mine."

"Thank you! Again I would like to speak."

The stranger was once more standing to address everyone. "These stories are very much all the same. Each time opportunity flew away for the same reason. Each time it came to the procrastinator, bringing a good plan. Each time they hesitated, not saying, 'Right now is the best time to act.' How can we succeed that way?"

"My friend, you speak wisely," responded the buyer. "Good luck fled from procrastination in both these tales. Yet, this isn't unusual. The spirit of procrastination is within all. We want riches, but often when an opportunity appears right in front of us, that spirit of procrastination from within urges us to delay acceptance.

"In procrastinating, we become our own worst enemies. In my younger days, I didn't know the action by that long word: I just thought my own poor judgment caused me to lose many profitable trades. Later in life, I attributed it to my stubborn nature. In the end, I recognize it for what it is – a habit of needless delaying when action is required, prompt and decisive action. I hated it when I finally came to this realization of what had been holding me back from success. That was when I was determined never to make the same mistakes again."

"Thank you! I would like to ask the merchant a question," said the stranger. "You wear fine robes, not like the rags that poor people wear. You speak like you have been successful in business. Tell us, do you listen now when procrastination whispers in your ear?"

"Like our friend the buyer, I also had to recognize and conquer procrastination," the merchant responded. "To me, it proved to be an enemy, always watching and waiting to trounce my accomplishments. The tale I told is only one of many similar stories I could tell to show how it drove away my opportunities. It isn't difficult to conquer, once you understand it. No one willingly permits a thief to rob their home. Nor does anyone willingly permit an enemy to drive away their customers and rob themselves of profits. When I finally recognized that my actions or lack of action were my enemy, I conquered it. Everyone has to master their spirit of procrastination before they can expect to share in the rich treasures of Babylon.

"What do you think, Arkad? Because you are the richest person in Babylon, many say you are also the luckiest. Do you agree with me that no one can achieve their full measure of success until they have completely crushed the spirit of procrastination within them?"

"It's as you say," Arkad admitted. "During my long life, I have watched generation following generation, marching forward along those avenues of trade, science, and learning that lead to success in life. Opportunities came to all these people. Some grasped theirs and moved steadily to the gratification of their deepest desires. But the majority hesitated, faltered, and fell behind."

Arkad turned to the cloth weaver. "You suggested that we debate good luck. Let's hear your thoughts on the subject now."

"I see good luck in a different light now. I had thought of it as something very desirable that might happen to someone without any effort on their part. Now I realize that lucky happenings aren't the sort of thing one may attract to oneself. From our discussion, I learned that it's necessary to take advantage of opportunities to attract good luck to oneself. Therefore, in the future, I will endeavor to make the best of such opportunities as they come to me."

"You have grasped the truths brought forth in our discussion," Arkad replied. "Good luck, we find, often follows opportunity but seldom comes otherwise. Our merchant friend would have found good luck if she had accepted the opportunity that was presented to her. Likewise, our friend, the buyer, would have enjoyed good luck if he had completed the purchase of the flock and sold it at such a handsome profit.

"We started this discussion to find a way by which good luck could be encouraged to come to us. I feel that we've found the way. Both the tales illustrated how good luck follows opportunity. There is a truth that many similar stories of good luck won or lost couldn't change. It is this: good luck can be enticed by accepting opportunities.

Those who are eager to grasp opportunities for their betterment attract the Gods of Good Luck. The Gods of Good Luck are always ready to help people of action. It is action that leads you forward to the successes you desire."

PEOPLE OF ACTION ARE FAVORED BY GOOD LUCK.

CHAPTER 5
THE FIVE LAWS OF GOLD

"A bag heavy with gold or a clay tablet carved with words of wisdom: if you had a choice, which would you choose?"

By the flickering light from the fire of desert shrubs, the suntanned faces of the listeners gleamed with interest.

"The gold, the gold," chorused the twenty-seven.

Old Kalabab smiled knowingly.

"Listen," she resumed, raising her hand. "Hear the wild dogs out there in the night. They howl and wail because they are lean with hunger. Yet feed them, and what do they do? Fight and strut. Then fight and strut some more, giving no thought to tomorrow that will surely come.

"You are all the same as the wild dogs. I give you a choice between gold and wisdom, and what do you do? Ignore the wisdom and waste the gold. And when tomorrow comes, you will wail because you have no more gold.

Gold is reserved for those who know its laws and abide by them."

Kalabab drew her white robe close about her legs because a cool night wind was blowing.

"You have served me faithfully on our long journey. You have cared for my camels and toiled uncomplainingly across the hot sands of the desert. You have even bravely fought the robbers that tried to take my merchandise. Because of everything you have done for me, I will tell you tonight the tale of the five laws of gold, such a tale as you have never heard before.

"Listen, and pay close attention to what I'm about to tell you. If you can put what I'm about to tell you into action in the days that come, you will obtain enough gold to secure your futures."

She paused impressively. Above a canopy of blue, the stars shone brightly in the crystal clear skies of Babylon. Behind the group loomed their faded tents, tightly anchored against possible desert storms. Beside the tents were neatly stacked bales of merchandise covered with sheets. Nearby the camel herd sprawled in the sand, some chewing their dinner contentedly, others snoring peacefully.

"You have told us many good tales, Kalabab," said the chief packer. "We look to your wisdom to guide us in the days when our service with you will be over."

"I have told you of my adventures in strange and distant lands, but tonight I will tell you of the wisdom of Arkad."

"We've heard of him," acknowledged the chief packer, "because he was the richest person that ever lived in Babylon."

"He was the richest person because he was wise in the ways of gold. Wiser than anyone who had come before him. Tonight I will tell you of his great wisdom as it was told to me by Nomasira, his daughter, many years ago in Nineveh, when I was but a teenager.

"My employer and I had worked late into the night in the palace of Nomasira. I had helped my boss bring incredible bundles of fine rugs, each one to be tried by Nomasira until she found the color that satisfied her. Finally, at last, she was pleased and requested we sit with her and drink a delicate sour drink that smelled sweet and was warm in my stomach.

Then she told us this tale of the great wisdom of Arkad, her father, just as I will tell it to you.

"In Babylon, it's the custom, as you know, that the firstborn of wealthy families lives with their parents in expectation of inheriting the estate. Arkad disapproved of this custom. Therefore, when Nomasira reached adulthood he sent for the young woman and said to her:

'My daughter, I want you to inherit our estate. You must, however, first prove that you are capable of wisely handling it. Therefore, I challenge you to go out into the world and show your ability to acquire gold, and make yourself respected among all.

"'To start you off well, I will give you two things that I myself was denied when I started as a poor youth to build up a fortune.

"'First, I give you this bag of gold. If you use it wisely it will be the basis of your future success.

"'Second, I give you this clay tablet on which the five laws of gold are carved. These laws will bring you wealth and security if you incorporate them into your life.

"'Ten years from this day, come back to your mother and me and give us an account of yourself. We will make you the heir to our estate if you have proven yourself worthy. Otherwise, we will give our wealth to the priests as an offering so they may barter for our souls.'

"So Nomasira went forth to make her own way, taking her bag of gold, the clay tablet carefully wrapped in silk cloth, and the horse on which she rode.

"The ten years passed, and Nomasira, as she had agreed,

returned to the house of her mother and father, who provided a great feast in her honor, and to which they invited many friends and relatives. After the feast was over, the father and mother mounted their throne-like seats at one side of the great hall, and Nomasira stood before them to give an account of herself as she had promised.

"It was evening. The room was hazy with smoke from the wicks of the oil lamps that dimly lit it. Servants in white woven jackets and tunics fanned the humid air rhythmically with long-stemmed palm leaves. A stately dignity colored the scene. The husband of Nomasira and her two young children, with friends and other family members, sat on rugs behind her, eager to hear her history.

"'Father,' she began deferentially, 'I bow before your wisdom. Ten years ago, when I stood at the gates of adulthood, you told me to go forth and become a woman respected among all instead of remaining a child to your fortune.

"'You gave me liberally from your gold. You gave me liberally from your wisdom. Of the gold, alas! I must admit I was disastrous in handling it. It ran off from my inexperienced hands as a wild hare flees at the first opportunity from the youth who captures it.'

"The father smiled indulgently. 'Continue, my daughter. Your tale interests me in all of its details.'

"'I decided to go to Nineveh, as it was a growing city, believing that I might find opportunities there. I joined a group of travelers, a caravan, all heading the same way. Amidst its members, I made numerous friends. Two well-spoken travelers were among my new friends. They had a beautiful white horse as fast as the wind.

"'As we traveled, they told me that in Nineveh there was a wealthy gambler who owned a horse so fast that it had never been beaten. Its owner believed that no horse living could run with greater speed. This gambler was confident that he would bet any amount his horse would win in a race. My new friends said that compared to their horse, this gambler's horse was as slow as a donkey carrying a heavy load, and it could be beaten easily.

"'I was so excited about their plan that it didn't take much to convince me to join them when they offered to include me in the bet they planned to make.

"'Our horse was badly beaten, and I lost most of my gold.' The father laughed. 'Later, I discovered that the gambler and these two, who I had thought were friends, were all working together. My two friends travel with groups like mine, looking for victims to swindle. This scam taught me my first lesson in looking out for myself.

"'I soon learned another equally bitter lesson. In the caravan there was another youth whom I became friendly with. She was the daughter of wealthy parents and, like myself, traveling to Nineveh to find a fitting place to call home. Not long after our arrival, she told me that a merchant had died, and their shop, with all of its rich merchandise and customers, could be bought at a discounted price. She said we would be equal partners, but first, she had to return to Babylon to retrieve her gold. She persuaded me to purchase the shop with my gold and agreed that her gold would be used later to run the business.

"'She kept delaying her trip to Babylon. In the meantime, she turned out to be a very unskillful buyer and a foolish spender. I finally came to my senses and realized I would be better off without her. But unfortunately, I didn't come to that conclusion before the business had deteriorated to where we had merchandise that nobody wanted to buy and no gold to buy better goods. So I sold what was left of the business to a merchant for next to nothing.

"'After this ordeal followed the most bitter days of my life. I tell you, my father, I'm not exaggerating. I looked for work but couldn't find any, because I wasn't trained in any skill that could enable me to earn. So I sold my horse and then became so desperate I had to sell my extra robes to have food and a place to sleep, but each day I could feel the cold wind of hunger and its big sister, starvation, blowing stronger.

"'But in those dark days, I remembered the confidence you and mother had in me. You had sent me out to become a self-sufficient adult, and I was determined to achieve that goal.' Tears formed in the parents' eyes. "'It was only at this time that I remembered the tablet that you had given to me – the tablet on which you had carved the five laws of gold. I stopped to read your words of wisdom and realized that if I had looked for wisdom first, I wouldn't have lost my gold.

"'I learned each law by heart and was determined that when good fortune smiled upon me again, I would be guided by the wisdom of age and not by the inexperience of youth.

"'For the benefit of all of you who are seated here tonight, I will read the words of wisdom my father engraved on the clay tablet which he gave me ten years ago:

1. "'Gold comes easily and will increase in quantity to those who will put aside at least one-tenth of their earnings to create wealth for their future and their family.
2. "'Gold works hard and happily for those who find wise investments, multiplying like rabbits in a pen.
3. "'Gold will stay with those who are cautious and protect it using the sound advice of the wise people who are employed to handle it.
4. "'Gold will slip away from those who invest in businesses or schemes that they aren't familiar with or invest in people who aren't skilled in using or earning gold.
5. "'Gold will run from those who would try to force impossible earnings, who follow the alluring advice of

tricksters and scammers, or who trust it to their own inexperienced investment skills.

"'These are the five laws of gold as written by my father. I proclaim these five laws are of greater value than gold itself, as you will see from the end of my tale.'

"Nomasira again faced her mother and father. 'I have told you of the depth of the poverty and despair that my inexperience brought me.

"'However, I believe there is no series of disasters that won't at some point come to an end. Mine came when I secured employment as a laborer, working to build the new outer wall of the city.

"'Gaining from my knowledge of the first law of gold, I saved a copper from my first pay, adding to it at every opportunity until I had a piece of silver. It was a slow process, for one must live. So I spent hesitantly on both food and shelter because I was determined to earn back as much gold as you, father, had given to me, before the ten years were over.

"'One day, the chief foreperson, with whom I had become quite friendly, said to me: "You are a thrifty youth who doesn't spend frivolously what you've earned. Do you have gold that you have set aside that is sitting idle? Does it earn you a return?"

"'Yes, it's idle,' I replied, 'But it's my great desire for it to accumulate gold to replace the gold my father gave – the gold I lost.'

"""That's a worthy goal," the foreperson agreed, "And tell me: do you know that the gold that you have saved can work for you and earn you even more gold?"

"'Unfortunately, my experience has been sad, because my father's gold has left me, and I fear that my current savings may do the same.'

"""If you have confidence in me, I will give you a lesson in the profitable handling of gold," the foreperson replied. "Within a year, the outer wall will be complete and ready for the great gates of bronze that will be built at each entrance to protect the city from the king's enemies.

""'In all Nineveh, there isn't enough metal to make these gates, and the king hasn't secured it. So here is my plan: a group of us will pool our gold and send a caravan to the copper and tin mines, which are far from here, and bring the metal for the gates back to Nineveh. Then, when the king says, 'Make the great gates,' we will be the only ones able to supply the metal, and we will be able to charge a rich price that he will likely pay. If the king decides not to buy from us, we will still have the metal that's still in demand by the smiths and can be sold for a fair price.'"

"'In the foreperson's offer, I recognized an opportunity to abide by the third law and invest my savings under the guidance of those who are wise in the matters of gold. So I agreed to the proposal, and I am grateful I did. Our venture was a success, and the transaction greatly increased my small savings of gold.

"'In due time, I was accepted as a member of this same group in other ventures. They were people who were wise in the profitable handling of gold. They talked over each plan presented with great care before agreeing to it. They would take no chance on losing their principal or tying it up in unprofitable investments from which their gold couldn't be recovered. Foolish things like the horse race and the partnership I had entered with my inexperience wouldn't have even been considered by this group. They would have immediately pointed out the weaknesses.

"'Through my association with these investors, I learned to invest gold to bring profitable returns safely. As the years went on, my treasure increased more and more rapidly. As a result, I not only made back all that I had lost, but much more.

"'My early misfortunes, my trials, and my success all tested me. But, time and again, the wisdom of the five laws of gold has been proven to be true in every test. To those who don't know the five laws, gold won't come to them often, and it will go from them quickly. But to those who follow the five laws, gold will come to them and work dutifully to increase in number.'

"Nomasira stopped speaking and motioned to her employee in the back of the room. The servant brought three heavy leather bags forward one at a time. One of these Nomasira took and placed on the floor before her mother and father, addressing them again:

'You give me a bag of gold, Babylon gold. To replace it, I am returning to you a bag of Nineveh gold of equal weight. An equal exchange, as all would agree.

"'You also gave me a clay tablet inscribed with wisdom. Here, look, in its place, I am returning two bags of gold.' After saying this, Nomasira took the other two bags that were brought out and placed them on the floor in front of her mother and father.

"'I do this to prove to you how much greater I value your wisdom than I value your gold. Who can measure in bags of gold the value of wisdom? Without wisdom, gold is quickly lost by those who have it, but with wisdom, gold can be secured by those who don't have it, as these three bags of gold prove.

"'It gives me the deepest satisfaction to stand before you and mother and say that, because of your wisdom, I have been able to become rich and respected before all.'

"The father placed his hand fondly on the head of Nomasira. 'You have learned your lessons well, and we are indeed fortunate to have a daughter to whom we may entrust our wealth.'"

Kalabab stopped telling his story and looked critically at her listeners. "What do you think of this story of Nomasira?" she continued. "Who among you can go to your mother or father and give an account of wise handling of your earnings?

"I know what you would say: 'I have traveled far, learned a lot, worked hard, and earned a substantial amount of coins, yet I have saved little gold. Some I spent wisely, some I spent foolishly, and most I lost in unwise ways.'

"Do you think it's luck or fate that some people have much gold and others have none? If you believe this, you are mistaken.

"Those who have much gold are those who know the five laws of gold and live by their rule.

Because I learned these five laws in my youth and observed them, I have become a wealthy merchant. It wasn't because of some strange magic that I accumulated my wealth.

"Wealth that comes quickly can go just as fast.

Wealth that stays with its owner to be enjoyed and used to their satisfaction comes gradually because it's a child born of knowledge and persistence.

"To earn wealth is a small burden to those who are thoughtful. However, bearing that burden consistently from year to year accomplishes the final goal.

"The five laws of gold offer you a rich reward if you observe them. Each of these five laws is rich with meaning. Don't think that because my story was short, it wasn't deep with meaning. I know each law by heart because, in my youth, I could see their value and wouldn't be content until I knew them word for word.

~

THE FIRST LAW OF GOLD

"Gold comes easily and will increase in quantity to those who will put aside at least one-tenth of their earnings to create wealth for their future and for their family."

"Anyone who will set aside one-tenth of their earnings consistently and invest it wisely will surely create a valuable estate – an estate that will provide an income for them in the future and further guarantee security for their family if the Gods call them to the world of darkness. This law always says that gold comes easily to such a person. I can attest to the truth of this with my own life. The more gold I accumulate, the more quickly it comes to me and increases in quantity. This is because the gold which I save earns more. Just as yours will, and its earnings earn more, and this is the working out of the first law."

THE SECOND LAW OF GOLD

"Gold works hard and happily for those who find wise investments, multiplying like rabbits in a pen."

"Gold, indeed, is a willing worker. It's always eager to multiply when an opportunity presents itself.

To everyone who has gold savings set aside, opportunities will come for its most profitable use. As the years pass, it will surprisingly multiply itself."

THE THIRD LAW OF GOLD

"Gold will stay with those who are cautious and protect it using the sound advice of the wise people who are employed to handle it."

Gold, indeed, stays with the cautious owner, just as it runs away from the careless owner. Those who seek the advice of others who are wise in handling gold soon learn not to jeopardize their treasure, but to preserve their savings carefully and to relish its consistent increase."

THE FOURTH LAW OF GOLD

"Gold will slip away from those who invest in businesses or schemes that they aren't familiar with or invest in people who are not skilled in using or earning gold."

Those who have gold yet aren't skilled in handling it will find many uses for it, which will seem profitable. But, most often, those uses are full danger of loss, and if properly analyzed by the wise, would show how small the possibility of profit is. Therefore, the inexperienced owner of gold who trusts their judgment and invests it in business or purposes with which they aren't familiar will often find they have made poor decisions. They pay with their treasure for their inexperience and education. Wise people invest their treasures with the advice of those skilled in the ways of gold."

THE FIFTH LAW OF GOLD

"Gold will run from those who would try to force impossible earnings, who follow the alluring advice of tricksters and scammers, or who put trust into their own inexperienced investment skills."

"Unbelievably fantastic investment opportunities will always come to the new owners of gold. These *opportunities* will excite you like an adventure story. They will make your treasure appear to have magical powers to earn ridiculous amounts of money if you only take advantage of these once-in-a-lifetime ventures to multiply your treasure many times over. Heed the wisdom of those who know the risks that lurk behind every plan to make extraordinary wealth quickly.

"Don't forget the wealthy investors of Nineveh who would not take the chance of losing their principal or tying it up in unprofitable investments."

"THIS ENDS my story of the five laws of gold. In telling it to you, I have given you the secrets of my success.

Yet, they aren't secrets but truths which everyone must first learn and then follow if they want to step out of the pack of those who worry each day about having enough food to eat or gold to pay for shelter.

"Tomorrow, we enter Babylon. Look! You can see the fire staying lit above the Temple of Bel! We are already in sight of the golden city. Tomorrow, each of you will have gold, the gold you have rightfully earned for your faithful services.

"Ten years from this night, what will you be able to say about this gold?

"Are there any among you who, like Nomasira, will use a portion of your gold to start an estate? Will you be, from this day and beyond, wisely guided by the wisdom of Arkad? Ten years from now, will it be a safe bet for me to think that one, or all of you, like the daughter of Arkad, will be rich and respected among all?

"Our wise actions follow us through life to assist and satisfy us, just as surely as our unwise actions follow us to plague and torment us. Unfortunately, neither can be forgotten. At the top of our list of torments are the memories of what we should have done. The opportunities that came to us and we didn't take.

"Babylon is rich with treasures, so rich no one can count their value in pieces of gold. Each year, they grow richer and more valuable. Like the treasures of every land, they are a reward, a rich reward awaiting those of purpose who are determined to secure their share.

"In the strength of your desires is a magical power. Guide this power with the knowledge of the five laws of gold, and you will share the treasures of Babylon."

CHAPTER 6

THE GOLD LENDER OF BABYLON

Fifty pieces of gold! Never had Rodan, the spear maker of old Babylon ever carried so much gold in his leather wallet. He strolled happily down the king's highway from the palace of the most generous royal family. Cheerfully the gold clinked as the wallet attached to his belt swayed with each step – it was the sweetest music he had ever heard.

Fifty pieces of gold! All his! He could hardly believe his good fortune. The power in those clinking metal coins! They could purchase anything he wanted, a grand house, land, cattle, camels, horses, chariots, whatever he might desire.

But what should he use it for? As he turned onto a side street towards the home of his sister, he could think of nothing he would want other than to possess those same glittering, heavy pieces of gold – all his to keep.

A few days later, as the moon made its first appearance in the sky, Rodan entered the shop of Zahra, the lender of gold and dealer in jewels and rare fabrics, with a perplexed look on his face. As he walked into the shop, he didn't slow down to look at the colorful articles artfully displayed. Instead, he passed straight through to the living quarters at the back. There he found the genteel Zahra lounging on a rug partaking of a meal.

"Would you spare a moment to provide me with some help, because I don't know what to do?" Rodan asked in a firm but friendly voice.

Zahra's narrow face smiled a friendly greeting. "What trouble have you gotten yourself into that you are seeking out the lender of gold at this hour? Have you been unlucky at the gaming table? Or has someone tricked you out of your coin in some other scheme? I have known you for many years, Rodan, and you have never requested my help before."

"No, no. Nothing like that. I don't need your gold. I seek your wise advice."

"Really! No! What is this? No one comes to the lender of gold for advice. My ears must be playing a trick on me."

"They hear just fine."

"Can this really be so? Rodan, the spear maker, displays more cleverness than all the rest, for he alone comes to Zahra, not for gold, but for advice. Many come to me for gold to pay for their mistakes, but as for advice, they never want what I would give them for free. Yet who is more able to advise than the lender of gold to whom so many come when they are in trouble?

"Eat with me, Rodan," she continued. "You will be my guest for the evening." She called her attendant, "Andol, please bring a rug for my friend, Rodan, the spear maker, who comes for advice. He will be my honored guest. Bring him food and get him my largest cup. Choose well of the best wine so that he will have satisfaction in drinking.

"Now, tell me, Rodan, what is it that troubles you?"

"It's the king's gift."

"The king's gift? The king gave you a gift, and that's the cause of your grief? What kind of gift did he give you?"

"THE KING WAS VERY pleased with the design I offered him for a new point on the spears of the royal guard. He was so pleased that he presented me with a gift of fifty pieces of gold, and now I am very confused.

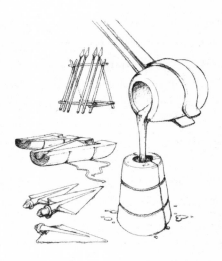

"I am called on hour after hour by those who have heard the news of my gift. They ask, beg, and plead that I share my gift with them."

"That's to be expected. There are more people who want gold than have it. Those who don't have it often want and sometimes feel entitled to the gold that has come to others easily as this gift has come to you. But that problem is easily solved. Can't you just say no? Is your will not as strong as your spears?"

"To most I can say no, yet sometimes I feel like it would be easier to say yes. Can I refuse to share with my own sister to whom I am deeply loyal?"

"Surely, your sister wouldn't want to deprive you of enjoying your reward."

"Her request is for her husband, Araman, who she wants to be a rich merchant. She feels that he has never had a chance, and she has asked me to loan him this gold so that he can become a prosperous merchant and repay me from his profits."

"My friend," resumed Zahra, "this is a worthy subject that you bring for us to discuss. Gold brings to its owners a responsibility and a changed position. It brings the fear that the owner may lose or be tricked away from what they own. It brings a feeling of power and the ability to do good. But, it also brings opportunities where its owners' good intentions may cause difficulties.

"Did you ever hear of the farmer from Nineveh who could understand the language of animals? I assume you haven't, since this isn't the kind of story to tell over firelight. But I will tell it to you now so that you will understand that there is more to borrowing and lending than passing gold from the hands of one to the hands of another.

"This farmer, who could understand what the animals said to each other, would stay in the farmyard each evening just to listen to their words. One evening she heard the ox complaining to the donkey about the challenges of his position: 'I work pulling the plow from morning until night. No matter how hot the day is, how tired my legs are, or how much the harness rubs my neck raw, I still have to work. But you are a creature of leisure. You are covered with a colorful blanket and do next to nothing except carry the farmer around wherever they want to go. When they stay at home, you rest and eat the green grass all day long.'

"Now, the donkey was a friendly sort and sympathized with the ox. 'My good friend', the donkey replied, 'you do work very hard, and I will help ease your troubles. I will tell you how you can have a day of rest. In the morning, when the workers come to hitch you to the plow, lie on the ground and cry out so much that they will say you are sick and can't work.'

"So the ox took the advice of the donkey, and the following day the workers returned to the farmer and said the ox was sick and couldn't pull the plow.

"'Then,' said the farmer, 'hitch the donkey to the plow, since the plowing must go on.'

"All that day, the donkey, who had only intended to help its friend, found itself compelled to do the ox's task. When night came, and it was released from the plow, it was resentful, and its legs were weak, and its neck was sore where the hitch had rubbed it raw.

"The farmer stayed back in the barnyard to listen again. The ox began first. 'You are my good friend. Because of your wise advice, I have enjoyed a day of rest.'

"'And I,' replied the donkey, 'am like many other soft-hearted fools who start to help a friend and end up doing their work for them. You pull your own plow from now on because if you don't, I heard the farmer tell the workers to send for the butcher if you ever get sick again. And I hope they do send for the butcher, because you are lazy.' That was the last time they spoke to one another – this ended their friendship. Can you tell me the moral to this tale, Rodan?"

"It's a good story," responded Rodan, "but I don't see the point of it."

"I didn't think you would. But it's there, and it's simple too. If you desire to help your friend, do so in a way that won't bring your friend's burdens onto yourself."

"I hadn't thought of that. It's a wise moral. Of course, I don't want to take on the burdens of my sister's husband. But tell me. You lend to many. Don't the borrowers repay you?"

Zahra smiled the smile of one whose soul is rich with much experience. "Should a loan be made if the borrower can't repay it? Shouldn't the lender be wise and judge carefully whether their gold can be put to good use by the borrower and then be returned. Or should the lender let their gold be wasted by someone who is unable to use it wisely, leaving the lender without their treasure and the borrower with an unpaid debt. I will show you the tokens in my token chest and let them tell you some of their stories."

Zahra got up and went to retrieve a chest as long as her arm, decorated with bronze designs. She placed it on the floor and squatted in front of it, resting both her hands on the lid.

"Each person who I lend to, I demand they leave me a token for my token chest, to remain with me until the loan is repaid. When they repay the loan, I give the token back, but if they never repay their loan, their token will always be a symbol and reminder of the borrower who didn't deserve my trust.

"My token box tells me the safest loans are to those whose possessions have a total value that is greater than the amount of gold they seek as a loan. They own lands, jewels, camels, or other things that could be sold to repay the loan. Some of the tokens given to me are jewels of more value than the loan. Others are promises that if the loan can't be repaid as agreed, they will deliver to me property to satisfy the loan. For loans that use property to secure my gold, I am guaranteed that my gold will be returned to me with the interest owed.

"Another type of borrower is the one who can *earn*. They are like you, Rodan, people who work or serve and are paid. They have income, and if they are honest and if there are no accidents that stop or slow their ability to work, I know that they also can repay the gold I loan them, and the interest to which I am entitled. Such loans are based on human effort.

"Others are those who have neither property nor guaranteed earning capacity. Life is hard, and some will always find hard times and gold in short supply. This is why I will only make these loans, no matter how small the amount requested, if they are guaranteed by good friends of the borrower, and if the friends consider them honorable. If the borrower can't repay it, the friend will, in order to keep their name and reputation in good standing."

Zahra released the clasp and opened the lid. Rodan leaned forward eagerly.

At the top of the chest sat a bronze bracelet. Zahra picked up the piece and touched it affectionately. "This, I believe, will always remain in my token chest because I fear the owner has passed on into the great darkness. I treasure this token as I treasure the memory of my good friend who placed it in my care. We worked and traded together in our youth with much success until one day he found a partner to wed – beautiful, but they weren't a good fit. My friend spent gold lavishly to gratify his partner's desires.

"He came to me in distress when his gold was gone. I counseled him. I told him I would help him to once more master his affairs. But it wasn't to be. After a great fight, the partner left him for another. In a fit of madness, he wandered off into the desert and hasn't been seen since."

"And the partner?" questioned Rodan.

"When last I heard the partner has also departed with someone new. This loan will never be repaid. Rodan, the chest tells you that people in an emotional state aren't safe risks for the gold lender.

"Here! Now, this is different." She reached for a ring carved from bone. "This belongs to a weaver and a farmer. I buy their rugs. The locusts came, and they had no food. So I helped them, and they repaid me when the new crop came. Later they came back and told me of some strange goats in a distant land as described by a traveler. These goats are supposed to have long hair, so fine and soft it could be woven into rugs more beautiful than any ever seen in Babylon. They wanted a herd, but they didn't have the money. So I lent them the gold to make the journey and bring back the goats. The farmer has taken good care of this new herd, and the weaver will surprise the people of Babylon with the most expensive and beautiful rugs that they would be lucky enough to buy. I will need to return this ring soon since they insist on repaying the loan early."

"Some borrowers do that?" questioned Rodan.

"If they borrow for purposes that will bring money back to them, I find that they do. But if they borrow because of their carelessness, I warn you to be cautious if you would like to see your lent gold back in your hand again."

"Tell me about this," Rodan requested, picking up a heavy gold bracelet inlaid with jewels in rare designs.

"Ah, you have interesting taste in jewelry, my good friend," joked Zahra.

"Just curious," retorted Rodan. "Just curious."

"Well, the owner of that piece of jewelry is an overprotective father who talks too much and says so little and drives me crazy. Once they had a lot of money and were good customers, but bad times came on them. He has a son whom he wanted to make into a merchant. So he came to me and borrowed gold so that the son could become a partner with a caravan owner who travels with his camels, trading in one city what he buys in another.

"This partner turned out to be a scoundrel and a cheat. While they were in some distant city, he packed up early and left the poor boy alone without any money or friend to help him out. Maybe when the youth has grown to an adult, he will repay the loan, but until then, I will get no interest on it – only too much talk from the father. But I do admit the jewels were worth the value of the loan."

"Did this man ask for your advice as to the wisdom of the loan?"

"Quite the opposite. He had envisioned this son of his as a wealthy and influential man of Babylon. To suggest anything to the contrary would infuriate him. I knew the risk I was taking with this inexperienced boy, but the father offered this jeweled bracelet as security, so I didn't refuse him.

"This," continued Zahra, waving a bit of rope tied into a knot, "belongs to Nebatur, the camel trader. When he buys a herd larger than his funds allow, he comes to me and brings me this knot, and I lend to him according to his needs. He is a wise trader. I have confidence in his good judgment and can lend to him without worrying. Many other merchants of Babylon have my confidence because of their honorable behavior. Their tokens come and go frequently in my token box. Good merchants are an asset to our city, and it profits me to help them to keep trade moving so that Babylon can be prosperous."

Zahra picked out a beetle carved out of turquoise and tossed it disdainfully onto the floor. "A bug from Egypt. The child who owns this doesn't care if she ever repays my gold. When I reprimand her, she replies, 'How can I repay you when bad luck follows me? You have plenty more gold.' What can I do? The token belongs to her parents' – a worthy family of little means who promised me their land and herd to support their child's enterprises. At first, the youth found success, but she was careless and too impatient to gain great wealth. Her knowledge was immature. Her business failed. Youth is ambitious. Youth too often tries to take shortcuts to secure wealth quickly. Youth often borrows unwisely.

"The young who have never had much experience can't realize that hopeless debt is like a bottomless pit that you can fall into quickly and where you may struggle to escape. It's a pit of sorrow and regrets where clouds hide the sun's brightness, and the night is made unhappy by sleeplessness. Even so, I don't discourage borrowing gold. In fact, I encourage it. I recommend borrowing if it's for a wise purpose. I myself made my first real success as a merchant with borrowed gold.

"But what should I do? This youth feels hopeless and accomplishes nothing. She is discouraged and makes no effort to earn or to repay. It's my right to take the family's land and cattle that was promised to me, but my heart doesn't want to take from the parents to pay for the child."

"All of this is very interesting," interrupted Rodan, "but I still don't have an answer to my question. Should I lend my fifty pieces of gold to my sister's husband? As you know, my family is dear to me."

"Your sister is an exceptional woman whom I admire. But if her husband were to come to me and ask to borrow fifty pieces of gold, I would ask him what he planned to use it for.

"If he answered that he hoped to become a shopkeeper like myself and deal in jewels and rich furnishings, I would ask, 'What knowledge do you have of this business? Do you know where you can buy at the lowest cost? Do you know where you can sell at a fair price?' Could he say yes to these questions?"

"No, he couldn't," Rodan admitted. "He has helped me in making spears, and he has helped in the shops, but not enough to say he understands the business of sales."

"Then I would tell him that his venture isn't wise. Retailers must learn their trade. His ambition, while worthy, isn't enough, nor is it practical, and I wouldn't lend him any gold.

"But, let's say for argument sake he said, 'Yes, I have helped shopkeepers. I know how to travel to the east and buy the rugs the weavers weave at a low cost. I also know many of the rich people of Babylon to whom I can sell these rugs at a large profit.' Then I would say, 'Your venture is wise and your ambition honorable. I will be glad to lend you the fifty pieces of gold if you can give me some guarantee that my gold will be returned to me.' But would he say, 'I have no security other than that I am an honorable soul, and I will pay you interest for the loan.' Then would I reply, 'I treasure each piece of my gold too much. If robbers were to take my gold from you as you traveled east, or take the rugs from you as you returned, then you would have no means of repaying me, and my gold would be gone forever.'

"Gold, you see, Rodan, is the merchandise of the lender of money. It's easy to lend. If it's lent unwisely, then it's difficult to get back. The wise lender doesn't want to take on the risk of the borrower's venture, but rather the guarantee of safe repayment.

"'It's good," Zahra continued, "to help those who are in trouble; it's good to help those whose fate has been back luck. It's good to help those who are just getting started so that they may progress and become valuable citizens. But help must be given wisely. If it isn't, you may end up like the farmer's donkey. In our desire to help, we take other people's burdens upon ourselves.

"Again, I've wandered from your question, Rodan, but hear my answer: keep your fifty pieces of gold. What you worked for earns you gold, and what was given to you as a reward is also yours. No one can claim what is yours. They may ask, beg, or demand your gold, but only you can say when you should let your gold go. If you would lend it so that it may earn you more gold, then lend with caution and in many places. I don't like gold to be idle, but I like risks even less. How many years have you worked as a spear maker?"

"Three years this month."

"How much, besides the king's gift, have you saved?"

"Three gold pieces."

"So, for each year that you have worked, you have denied yourself good things to save from your earnings one piece of gold?"

"That's right."

"Then would it not have taken you fifty years of labor and fifty years of self-denial to save fifty pieces of gold?"

"Yes, that would be a lifetime of labor."

"Do you think your good sister would want you to jeopardize the savings of fifty years of labor so that her husband might experiment with being a shopkeeper?"

"Not if I put it to her in those terms."

"Then go and say to your sister, 'For three years, I have worked each day except the weekend, from morning to night, and I have denied myself many things that my heart craved. For each year of hard work and self-denial, I have one piece of gold to show for my efforts. You are my sister, and I love you dearly. I hope your husband will engage in business and be a great success. If he provides me with a plan that seems wise and possible to me and my friend, Zahra, then I will gladly lend him my savings of an entire year, one gold coin, not fifty, so that he may have an opportunity to prove that he can succeed.' If he has what it takes within him to succeed, then he can prove it. If he fails, he won't owe you more than he can hope to repay someday.

"I am a gold lender because I own more gold than I need to sustain myself. I want my extra gold to work for others and, by doing so, earn me more gold. I have worked hard and denied myself many things to secure my gold, so I don't want to take a risk that might cause me to lose it. That's why I will no longer lend any of it if I am not confident that it's safe and will be returned to me. Nor will I lend it when I am not convinced that what it has earned in interest will be promptly paid to me.

"I have told you, Rodan, a few of the secrets of my token chest so that you may understand the weakness of people and their eagerness to borrow what they don't have the ability to repay. From my tokens, you can see how often borrowers have high hopes of making great earnings if they only had gold. But you can also see how those hopes fall flat when they don't have the ability or training to achieve their goals.

"You, Rodan, now have gold which you should start using to earn more gold for yourself. You are about to become a gold lender just as I am. If you can safely preserve your treasure, it will produce considerable earnings for you and be a rich source of pleasure and profit for all of your days. But if you let it escape, it will be a source of constant sorrow and regret as long as you live.

"What do you desire the most of the gold in your wallet?"

"To keep it safe."

"Wisely spoken," replied Zahra approvingly. "Your first desire is for safety. Would your gold be truly safe from possible loss in your sister's husband's hands?"

"I fear it wouldn't. He isn't wise in guarding gold."

"Then don't be persuaded by foolish feelings of obligation to trust your treasure to any person. If you want to help your family or friends, find other ways other than risking the loss of your treasure. Don't forget that gold slips away in unexpected ways from those who are unskilled in guarding it.

"Other than safety, what do you desire of your treasure?"

"That it earns more gold."

"Again, you speak with wisdom. It should be made to earn and grow larger. Gold wisely lent may double itself with its earnings before you grow old. If you risk losing it, you risk losing all that it would have earned as well.

"Therefore, don't be persuaded by the fantastic plans of impractical people who think they see ways to force your gold to make impractical earnings. Such plans are the creations of dreamers who are unskilled in the safe and dependable laws of trade. Be conservative in what you expect your gold to earn so that you can keep and enjoy your treasure. To lend it out with a promise of unrealistic returns is to invite loss.

"Seek out and associate yourself with people and businesses who have a history of success. Under their mentorship, your treasure may find opportunities to earn and be secure. By the use of their wisdom and experience, you may avoid mistakes that often follow those who have been given a gift of gold."

When Rodan tried to thank Zahra for her wise advice, she wouldn't listen, saying, "The king's gift will teach you wisdom. If you want to keep your fifty pieces of gold, you must be discreet. Many uses will tempt you. Much advice will be given to you. Numerous opportunities to make large profits will be offered. The stories from my token box should warn you that before you let any piece of gold leave your pouch, you should be sure that you have a safe way to pull it back again. If you would like more of my advice, please return. I will be glad to give it.

"'Before you go, Rodan, read this passage that I have carved beneath the lid of my token box. It applies equally to the borrower and the lender.'"

> BETTER A LITTLE CAUTION THAN A GREAT
> REGRET.

CHAPTER 7
THE WALLS OF BABYLON

Opis and Ishtar had seen this happen before, but they never thought they would be the ones to lose a dear friend. Banzar had accompanied them to the halls of learning, where they sat and listened to the teachings of Arkad, the richest person in Babylon. They had visited him many times since hearing those teachings, and as sure as the walls of Babylon secure the city, their wealth had started to grow as Arkad had insisted it would.

But now, they sat solemnly reminiscing about days gone by. They had been instructed to protect their savings from loss and ensure an income in the future, but not enough time had passed for them to reap all of the rewards of their newly growing wealth. And now, only a few short years after receiving the teachings, their friend had been called to the other realm by the Gods. Their friend's family was left with less income to pay the many accumulating bills.

Being as close as siblings, they were happy to support Banzar's family as best they could, but that could only go so far. They had their own families to consider.

"We must protect ourselves and our wealth like the soldiers

protect the city from our enemies," said Opis. "I am happy to support Banzar's family, but there is only so much I can give without putting my family's well-being in jeopardy."

"I would also like to protect my wealth and ensure my family is well taken care of if I would meet the same fate as Banzar, but what can we do?" Ishtar replied. "No one knows when their time on this earth will cease."

"We should put money aside to protect our wealth, just as we do to grow our wealth."

"I envy you, Opis, if you have a flow of coins enough to put more of it away. I don't have much that I can spare. Even if I did, it takes time to build wealth, just as it would take time to protect it."

"Yes, but it only takes a moment to lose our wealth," Opis interrupted.

"We've just begun our journey to build wealth," said Ishtar. "I have diligently set no less than one coin out of every ten aside as we've been instructed. To protect ourselves against tragedy, I would need to build two fortunes. One to call my own and the other to protect it."

Opis's face lit up at this, and a surprising smile emerged. "You may not have enough wealth, but *we* do."

Ishtar tilted her head in puzzlement at this.

Opis continued. "What if we pooled our money? We both would contribute to a collaborative fund. We would have a more considerable sum than either one of us could create on our own."

"Then we would have a greater fortune but still not be protected," Ishtar asked.

"No, we wouldn't pool all of our fortunes together. You would still build your wealth, and I would build mine. But we would take some of what we earn to make a third fortune. We would use that third fortune if either one of us fell on hard times."

"This idea is clever, but with just the two, the sum of that fund would still be too small to protect us if we met tragedy tomorrow," said Ishtar. "Don't forget the wisdom of Arkad. To grow our wealth, we must build it slowly over time. Like the building of a wall, it must be done methodically. A wall isn't one massive brick, but many small bricks laid side by side and one on top of the others. So too should we build our wealth and the fortune to protect our wealth. It would take many years to build a third fortune, and I can't afford to put much more money aside than I already do."

"Yes, you are right. It would still be a small sum in a month or a year if only we could contribute more, but I am not any better off than you, Ishtar. If I continue to live by the teachings of Arkad, I would jeopardize my wealth tree or struggle if I started to use too much of the coin intended for our dinner table to protect my wealth."

"It's a shame that we didn't think of this idea when Banzar was still here. Banzar would have seen the genius of this plan and contributed to our pool of funds," Ishtar mused.

"Ishtar, you are wise, yet you don't know it! That is the solution! While this plan may be too late for Banzar, it isn't too late for the other citizens of Babylon. Are there no other people who would benefit from having their wealth protected?"

Opis continued. "While not all of the students who heard Arkad's teaching have followed his path, many have. And many of them will see the wisdom of this plan and contribute to the pool. With enough people contributing, the amount we would need to use our income would be so small as not to put our wealth or our families at risk. With enough people, this pool could be a small fortune in short order.

"If we collectively pool our money and manage it with investments so that it grows as wealth grows, then if any one of us needs to draw on it to repair a home, or bury a loved one, or supplement the income of that loved one, the coin will be there. "

"But won't drawing from this pool not deplete it?" asked Ishtar.

"A little, yes, but not enough to drain it. I doubt one or two families using the pool would have much effect on the pool's total sum. Since all members of this pool must contribute to it regularly, it will keep growing. It will also grow on its own accord if some of it is invested, and its earnings are made to multiply according to Arkad's teachings. It will replenish itself of anything that's taken from it."

"And why would only one or two families need it at a time? Couldn't a horde of families not seek to draw on it?"

"That's unlikely. Tragedy, while certain in everyone's life, rarely strikes many people all at once. Yes, Banzar has passed on, but you and I sit here alive and well. With a large enough pool of families, we spread the risk of tragedy amongst us all."

"So you say," Ishtar interrupted, "but if my home catches on fire, will it not spread to my neighbor too?"

"Yes, it will, but by then, the whole village will have turned out with a brigade of buckets and water to ensure it spreads no further. Again, if we can convince enough families of the soundness of this ideal, that tragedy could surely be absorbed by the fund and support you and your neighbors as you rebuild your homes.

"Today, if that fire is lit, the same damage would occur to our community, but all of the hard work you spent to build your home would be lost. However, with this insurance fund, your home, while lost, could be rebuilt, and you are made whole. To continue to nurture your wealth tree, rather than see it being burnt down to its roots."

"Then what are we waiting for? Let's go out today and find others to join the insurance fund and protect our wealth."

Babylon endured century after century because it was fully protected. It couldn't afford to be otherwise. Just as the walls of Babylon had repulsed many mighty and vicious foes determined to loot its rich treasures, so too do insurance, savings, and dependable investments guard against the unexpected tragedies that may enter any door and seat themselves before any fireside.

WE CAN'T AFFORD TO BE WITHOUT
ADEQUATE PROTECTION.

CHAPTER 8
THE CAMEL TRADER OF BABYLON

The hungrier one becomes, the clearer one's mind works – also, the more sensitive one becomes to the odors of food.

Tarkad, the daughter of Azure, certainly thought so. For two whole days she had tasted no food except two small figs snatched from a garden. She would have taken more if it wasn't for the angry gardener who yelled at her to "be gone" and chased her down the street. The farmer's harsh screams were still ringing in her ears as she walked through the marketplace. The memory of the chase and her shame kept her from attempting to pluck any more fruit from the tempting baskets in the market.

Never before had she realized how much food was brought to the markets of Babylon and how good it smelled. Leaving the market, she walked across to the inn and paced back and forth in front of the restaurant. Perhaps here she might meet someone she knew, someone from whom she could borrow a copper that would get her a smile from the unfriendly keeper of the inn and, more importantly, some food. Without the copper, she knew how unwelcome she would be.

She was so deep in thought she unexpectedly found herself face to face with the one person she wished most to avoid, the tall, bony figure of Dabasir, the camel trader. Of all the people she had borrowed money from, Dabasir made her feel the most uncomfortable about not repaying quickly enough what she had borrowed.

Dabasir's face lit up at the sight of her. "Ah! It's Tarkad, just the one I wanted to see. Now you won't have to find me to repay the two pieces of copper I lent you a month ago, or the piece of silver I lent to you the month before that. How lucky for me, since I could make good use of those coins today. Well, where are my coins?"

Tarkad stuttered, and her face flushed. She didn't have the energy to argue with Dabasir, but she also had no money to speak of. "I am sorry, very sorry," she mumbled weakly, "but I don't have the copper nor the silver with which I could repay."

"Then get it," Dabasir insisted. "Surely you can get your hands on a few coppers and a piece of silver to repay the generosity of your old family friend who helped you when you were in need?"

"'Sorry. If it weren't for all of the bad luck I have had lately, I would have the coins to repay you."

"Bad luck! You blame the Gods for your laziness. Bad luck follows anyone who focuses more on borrowing than on repaying. Come with me while I eat. I am hungry, and I want to tell you a story."

Tarkad flinched from the harshness of Dabasir, but at least this was an invitation to enter the restaurant.

Dabasir gestured to the far corner of the room where they seated themselves on small rugs.

When Kauskor, the owner, appeared, smiling, Dabasir said with his usual freedom, "Kauskor, you old dog of the desert, I am starving. Bring me a leg of goat, brown with gravy, and bread and vegetables. And don't forget my friend here. Bring her a jug of water. Have it cooled, for the day is hot."

Tarkad's heart sank. Must she sit here and drink water while she watched this man devour an entire goat leg? She couldn't think of anything to say, so she said nothing.

Dabasir, however, didn't care for silence. He continued smiling and waving his hand good-naturedly to the other customers, all of whom knew him.

"I hear from a traveler who just returned from Urfa of a certain jewel collector who has a piece of stone cut so thin that you can look through it. They put it in the window of their house to keep out the rain. It's yellow, so this traveler says, and he was permitted to look through it, and all the outside world looked strange and not like it really is. What do you think of that, Tarkad? Do you think the world could look a different color from what it really is?"

"I suppose, maybe," responded Tarkad, who was much more interested in the fat leg of goat placed before Dabasir.

"Well, I know it's true since I once saw the world colored very differently. Let me tell you a story about how I came to see things in their right color."

"Dabasir is going to tell a story," whispered a neighboring diner to his neighbor and dragged his rug closer. Other diners brought their food over and crowded in a semi-circle. They chewed noisily in the ears of Tarkad and brushed her with their greasy fingers. She alone sat without food, and Dabasir didn't offer to share any with her. He didn't even offer her the small corner of hard bread that had fallen from the platter to the floor.

"The story that I am about to tell," began Dabasir, pausing to bite a chunk from the goat leg, "relates to my early life and how I became a camel trader. Did anyone of you know that I once was a criminal in Syria?"

A murmur of surprise ran through the audience. Dabasir sat back and listened with satisfaction.

"When I was a young man," continued Dabasir after another vicious bite on the goat leg, "I learned the trade of my family, making saddles. I worked in the family shop and eventually met my partner.

"Being young and not very skilled, I was able to earn only a little bit. Just enough to support my new family in a modest way. I craved the good things that I couldn't afford. But soon I found that the shopkeepers would trust me to pay later even though I couldn't pay at the time. Being young and inexperienced, I didn't know that by spending more than I earned, I was planting the seeds of needless self-indulgence from which I would only reap trouble and humiliation. So I indulged my whims for fine clothing. I bought expensive gifts for my wife and our home that were beyond our ability to pay.

"I paid when I could, and for a while, everything was fine. But after some time, I discovered I couldn't use my earnings to live on and pay my debts. The shopkeepers, who were my creditors, began to hound me to pay for my extravagant purchases, and my life became miserable. I borrowed from my friends but couldn't repay *them* either. Things went from bad to worse. Finally, my wife returned to her parents, and I decided to leave Babylon and look for another city where I might have better opportunities.

"For two years, I had a troubled and unsuccessful life working for caravan traders, who would travel from city to city trading. When I was with the caravan, I met robbers who were friendly to me. These robbers would search the desert for unguarded caravans. I knew that to rob was wrong and unworthy of the son of my parents, but I was seeing the world through a colored stone and didn't realize how far I had fallen into disgrace.

"We were successful on our first trip, capturing a rich load of gold and silks and valuable merchandise. This loot we took to the city and wasted.

The second time, we weren't so fortunate. Just after we had taken our loot, we were attacked by the guards of a native tribe whom the caravans paid for protection. We were taken to Damascus, where we stood for a brief trial, were found guilty, and sentenced to unpaid labor.

"Being a reckless youth, I thought everything was a joke until all that I owned was taken from me. I had nothing but some clothes to cover me. I was sent into the desert to work, as a prisoner, for a tribal chief. It was only then that I realized the hopelessness of my situation. The chief had enough laborers and didn't know what to do with me. Finally, he decided to give me to his wife, to use me if she wanted.

"I stood frozen in front of this woman, as she would be the one who would determine my fate. I wondered if I could expect pity from her. Sira seemed forty, maybe fifty years old, and she looked at me with no expression in her eyes.

It felt like days that I stood waiting for her to decide. Then, finally, Sira spoke up in a cold voice.

"'We have too many laborers and too few camel tenders. Today, if I could, I would visit my mother, who is sick with a fever. Yet there is no one I trust to lead my camel. Ask this prisoner if he can lead a camel.'

"The chief questioned me, 'What do you know about camels?'

"Struggling to conceal my eagerness, I replied, 'I can make them kneel, I can load them, I can lead them on long trips without tiring. And if needed, I can repair their harness and saddles.'

"'The criminal seems to have the needed skills, Sira. If you want, take the prisoner as your camel tender.'

"So I was turned over to Sira, and that same day I led her camel on a long journey to her sick mother. I took the opportunity to thank her for taking pity on me and also to tell her that I wasn't a criminal. I was once an honorable saddle maker in Babylon. I also told her most of my story. What she said to me afterwards unsettled me. And I've thought about it long and hard since.

"'How can you call yourself honorable when your actions brought you to this? If someone has the soul of a criminal in them, won't they become a criminal no matter what they were at birth? But, on the other hand, if someone has within them the soul of an honorable citizen, won't they become respected and honored in their community despite their misfortune?'

"For over a year, I worked and lived with the prisoners, but I didn't feel like I was one of them. Then, one day Sira asked me, 'In the evening when the other criminals can socialize and enjoy each other's company, why do you sit alone in your tent?'

"To that I responded, 'I am pondering what you said to me. I wonder if I have the soul of a criminal. I don't want to be a criminal, so I can't join them, and so I sit alone.'

"'I, too, must sit alone,' she confided. 'My dowry was large, and my husband married me because of it. Yet he doesn't care about me, nor do I care about him. Because of this and because I have no children, family, or friend to keep my company, I sit alone.'

"'What do you think of me?' I asked her suddenly. 'Do I have the soul of someone of honor or do I have the soul of a criminal?'

"'Do you want to repay the debts you owe in Babylon?' she asked.

"'Yes, I want to, but I don't see a way.'

"'If you happily let the years slip by and make no effort to repay, then you have the soul of a criminal. No one can be respected if they don't respect themselves to repay the debts they owe.'

"'But what can I do while I am your prisoner?'

"'You are a prisoner, and you will remain one as long as you are weak.'

"'I am not weak,' I denied hotly.

"'Then prove it.'

"'How?'

"'Doesn't the kingdom fight all its enemies in every way it can and with all the force it has? Your debts are your enemies. They ran you out of Babylon. You left them alone, and they grew too strong for you. If you had fought them, you could have conquered them and been one honored among the townspeople. But you didn't have the strength to fight them, and look what it has cost you. Because you were too weak to fight, you are now my prisoner.'

"I thought over Sira's unkind words and tried to think of how I would defend myself from her claims. I wanted to explain to her that I was honorable. I would have told her I wasn't a criminal at heart, but I didn't have the chance. Three days later, Sira's maid took me to her.

"'My mother is very sick again,' she said. 'Saddle the two best camels in my husband's herd. Tie on water skins and saddlebags for a long journey. The maid will give you food at the kitchen tent.' So I packed the camels, wondering all the while why the maid was providing so many provisions, for the mother lived less than a day's journey away. The maid rode the rear camel, which followed, and I led the camel of my mistress. When we reached her mother's house, it had just turned dark. Sira dismissed the maid and said to me,

'Dabasir, do you have the soul of an honorable man or the soul of a criminal?'

"'The soul of an honorable man,' I insisted.

"'Now is your chance to prove it. Take these camels and be free. I release you from my custody. Here in this bag are some clothes, and I will make a gift of these camels to you.'

"'You have the soul of a queen,' I told her. 'I hope you also find happiness.'

"'Happiness,' she responded, 'doesn't await the runaway wife who looks for it in far lands among strange people. Go your own way, and may the Gods of the desert protect you, because the route is far and there is no food or water.'

"I needed no further urging, so I thanked her warmly and was away into the night. I didn't know this strange country and had only a faint idea of the direction in which Babylon lay, so I struck out bravely across the desert toward the hills. I rode one camel and the other I led. All that night and the next day I traveled, and all the next day as well, urged on by the knowledge that this new freedom that Sira had provided me might not be what the tribal chief wanted, and that he might consider me an escapee. If that were the case, I knew my freedom would be short if I didn't make it back to Babylon.

"Late that afternoon, I reached a rough country as uninhabitable as the desert. The sharp rocks bruised the feet of my faithful camels, and soon they were picking their way slowly and painfully along. As I travelled, I saw no one, not even an animal, and I understood why. There was nothing here for anyone or anything to survive on. I would have avoided it, too, if I had the choice.

"It was such a miserable journey from that point on that very few people would have lived to tell about it. Day after day, we plodded along. Our food and water ran out. The heat of the sun was relentless. At the end of the ninth day, I slid from the back of my camel with the feeling that I was too weak ever to remount and I would surely die, lost in this abandoned land.

"I stretched out on the ground and slept. I didn't wake until the first gleam of daylight.

"I sat up and looked around. There was a coolness in the morning air. My camels lay not far away from me, looking sad and depressed. All around me was a barren land covered with rock and sand and thorny things, no sign of water or anything to eat for my camels or me.

"Could it be that I would face my end in this empty wasteland? My mind was clearer than it had ever been before. My body now seemed of little importance. My parched and chapped lips, my dry and swollen tongue, my empty stomach all had lost the importance that they had held the day before.

"I looked across into the uninviting distance, and once again the question came to me. 'Do I have the soul of a criminal or the soul of an honorable man?' Then with clearness, I realized that if I had the soul of a criminal, I should give up, lie down in the desert and give up, a fitting end for a criminal.

"But if I had the soul of an honorable man, what then? I would force my way back to Babylon, repay the people who had trusted me, bring happiness to my wife who truly loved me, and bring peace and contentment to my parents.

"'Your debts are your enemies who have run you out of Babylon,' Sira had said. Yes, this was true. So why had I refused to stand my ground and fight to keep my honor? Why had I brought shame on my family?

"Then a strange thing happened. All the world seemed to be of a different color, as though I had been looking at it through a colored stone that was suddenly removed. At last I saw the true values of life.

"Die in the desert? Not me! With a new vision, I saw what I had to do. First I had to go back to Babylon and face everyone I owed an unpaid debt. I would tell them that after years of wandering and misfortune, I had come back to pay my debts as fast as the Gods would permit. Next, I would make a home for my wife and make my parents proud of the citizen I'd become.

"My debts were my enemies, but the people I owed were my friends since they had trusted me and believed in me.

"I staggered weakly to my feet. Who cares about hunger? Who cares about thirst? They were minor obstacles on the road to Babylon. Within me surged the soul of an honorable man going back to conquer his enemies and reward his friends. I was motivated like never before.

"The eyes of my camels brightened at the new energy in my voice. With great effort, and after a few attempts, they got back to their feet. They pushed on toward the north, where something within me said we would find Babylon.

"We found water. We passed into a more fertile country where we found grass and fruit. We found the trail to Babylon because the soul of an honorable person looks at life as a series of problems to be solved and solves them, while the soul of a criminal whines, 'What can I do? I'm only a criminal.'

"How about you, Tarkad? Does your empty stomach make your thoughts clear? Are you ready to take the road that leads back to self-respect? Can you see the world in its true color? Do you want to pay back your debts, all of your debts, and once again be honorable and respected in Babylon?"

Tears came to the eyes of the youth. She rose eagerly to her knees. "You have shown me a vision; I already feel the soul of an honorable woman surging inside of me."

"But how did you do when you returned to Babylon?" questioned an interested listener.

"When you are determined, a way can be found," I replied.

"I now had the determination, so I set out to find a way. First, I visited everyone I was indebted to and begged for more time to earn enough to repay them. Most of them were glad to give me some extra time. Several cursed me, and others offered to help me. One friend gave me the very help I needed. It was Zahra, the gold lender. After learning that I had been a camel tender, she sent me to old Nebatur, the camel trader, just commissioned by our good king to purchase many herds of sound camels for the great expedition. With him, I was able to put my knowledge of camels to good use and earn a wage. Gradually I was able to repay every copper and every piece of silver. Then, at last, I could hold up my head and feel that I was honorable among our fellow citizens."

Again Dabasir turned to his food. "Kauskor, you snail," he shouted loudly enough to be heard in the kitchen, "the food is cold. Bring me more meat fresh from the fire. And bring a large portion for Tarkad; the daughter of my oldest friend is hungry and will eat with me."

That's how the story of Dabasir, the camel trader of old Babylon, ended. He found his soul when he realized a great truth, a truth that had been known and used by the wise long before his time.

It has led people of all ages out of difficulties and into success. It will continue to do so for those who have the wisdom to understand its magic power. It's for anyone to use who reads these lines.

WHEN YOU ARE DETERMINED, A WAY CAN BE FOUND.

CHAPTER 9

THE CLAY TABLETS FROM BABYLON

---------- Email Message ---------
From: Ellis Johnson <Ellis.Johnson@clearviewuniversity.org>
Date: Thurs, May 9, 2019 at 10:05 AM
Subject: Re: Clay Tablets from Babylon?
To: Morgan Caldwell <Morgan.Caldwell@linwellmuseum.org>

Hello Prof. Caldwell,
The five uncategorized clay tablets you recently re-discovered in the museum's vaults have arrived safely. Upon inspection, I can confirm that the writing is indeed cuneiform and that the tablets must have been excavated from the ruins of Babylon. I have found them fascinating and have genuinely enjoyed translating their inscriptions. Sorry for the delay in replying to your email but I wanted to wait until the translations were done (see attached).

The tablets arrived undamaged: thanks for packing them so carefully.

I'm sure you'll be as surprised as we in the laboratory were at the story they tell. You expect the dim and distant past to be all about romance and adventure. *Arabian Nights* sort of thing. But when instead it is about the problems that a person named Dabasir has in paying off his debts, you realize that the conditions of the ancient world haven't changed as much in five thousand years as we might have thought.

It's odd, you know, but these old inscriptions have me feeling a bit "basic," as the students say. As a college prof, I'm supposed to be a thinking human possessing a working knowledge of most subjects. Yet, here comes this person out of the dust-covered ruins of Babylon to offer a way I had never heard of to pay off my debts and at the same time acquire money to jingle in my wallet.

It will be interesting to see whether it will work as well nowadays as in old Babylon. My partner and I plan to try it out on our finances, which could be improved.
Good luck with this valuable work, and I'm happy to help again any time.

Best Regards,

Ellis Johnson
Department of Archaeology
St. Catharine's College
Clearview University
Burleigh Hill, CA
Ellis.Johnson@clearviewuniversity.org

Attachements:
Translated Clay Tablets No. I, II, III, IV, & V

TABLET NO. I

I, Dabasir, who have recently returned from captivity in Syria, am resolved to pay my many debts. I will do so with determination. Each time the moon is full, I will make a permanent record of my journey on clay to guide and assist me. This record will motivate me to carry through with my plan to become a person of means worthy of respect in my native city of Babylon.

With the wise advice of my good friend Zahra, the gold lender, I am determined to follow an exact plan that she says will lead any honorable person out of debt and into means and self-respect.

This plan includes three purposes which are my hope and desire.

First, the plan provides for my future prosperity.

Therefore one-tenth of all I earn will be set aside as mine to keep. Zahra shows her wisdom when she says:

"That person who keeps in their purse or wallet both gold and silver that they don't spend is good to their family and loyal to their king.

"The person who has only a few coppers in their purse or wallet is indifferent to their family and indifferent to their king.

"But the person who keeps nothing in their purse or wallet is unkind to their family and is disloyal to their king, for their heart is bitter.

"Therefore, the person who wants to achieve must have coins that they can keep to jingle in their wallet or purse, so that they have in their heart love for their family and loyalty to their king."

Second, the plan provides that I will support my wife, who has returned to me from her parents' home. Zahra says that to take good care of your family puts self-respect into your heart and adds strength and determination to your purpose.

Therefore, seven-tenths of all I earn will be used to support our home. It will help pay for the clothes we wear and the food we eat, with a bit extra to spend, so our lives aren't lacking in pleasure and enjoyment. But we must take great care that we don't spend more than seven-tenths of what we earn for these worthy purposes. That is the key to the success of the plan.

I must live on this portion and never use more nor buy what I can't pay for out of this portion.

~

TABLET NO. II

Third, the plan provides that I will pay my debts out of my earnings.

Therefore, each time the moon is full, two-tenths of all I have earned will be divided honorably and fairly among those who have trusted me and to whom I am indebted. In doing so, in due time, all my debts will be paid. Therefore, I engrave here the name of every person I am indebted to and the amount of my debt:

- Fahru, the cloth weaver, 2 silver, 6 copper
- Sinjar, the couch maker, 1 silver
- Ahmar, my friend, 3 silver, 1 copper
- Zankar, my friend, 4 silver, 7 copper
- Askamir, my friend, 1 silver, 3 copper
- Elham, the house owner, 14 silver
- Harinsir, the jewel maker, 6 silver, 2 copper
- Diarbeker, my father's friend, 4 silver, 1 copper
- Zahra, the gold lender, 9 silver
- Rabia, the farmer, 1 silver, 7 copper

(From here on, disintegrated and indecipherable.)

~

TABLET NO. III

TO THESE CREDITORS, I owe in total one hundred and nineteen pieces of silver and one hundred and forty-one pieces of copper. Because I owed this amount and saw no way to repay it, I left my wife and my native city to seek easy wealth elsewhere. But unfortunately, instead of seeking honest work, I found disaster as a criminal held captive in the desert.

Now that Zahra has shown me how I can repay my debts in small sums from my earnings, I realize the great extent of my folly in running away from the results of my extravagances. Therefore, I have visited my creditors and explained to them that I have no resources to pay except my ability to earn. I've told them I intend to apply two-tenths of all I make towards my debts and pay them evenly and honestly. This much I can pay but no more. Therefore, if they are patient with me, my obligations will be paid in full in time.

Ahmar, whom I thought my best friend, reviled me bitterly, and I left him in humiliation. Rabia, the farmer, pleaded that I pay her first as she badly needed help. Elham, the house owner, was disagreeable and insisted that she would make trouble for me unless I quickly settled in full with her.

All the rest willingly accepted my proposal. Therefore, I am more determined than ever to carry through, convinced that it's easier to pay one's debts than to avoid them. Even though I can't meet the needs and demands of a few of my creditors, I will deal fairly with them all.

～

TABLET NO. IV

Again the moon shines full. I have worked hard with a free mind. My good wife has supported my intentions to pay my creditors. Because of our wise determination, I have earned nineteen pieces of silver during the past moon, buying camels of sound wind and good legs for Nebatur.

This I have divided according to the plan. One-tenth, I set aside to keep as my own; seven-tenths is used by my wife and me to pay for our living; and two-tenths are divided among my creditors as evenly as could be done in coppers.

I didn't see Ahmar but left it with his wife. Rabia was so pleased she offered to kiss my hand. Old Elham alone was grouchy and said I must pay faster. All the others thanked me and spoke well of my efforts.

Therefore, at the end of one moon, my debt is reduced by almost four pieces of silver, and I also possess nearly two pieces of silver, upon which no one can claim. My heart is lighter than it has been for a long time.

Again the moon shines full. I have worked hard but with poor success. I have been able to buy only a few camels. I have only earned eleven pieces of silver. Nevertheless, my good wife and I have stood by the plan even though we've bought no new clothing and eaten little but vegetables as we couldn't afford meat.

Again I paid ourselves one-tenth of the eleven pieces while we lived on seven-tenths. I was surprised when Ahmar commended my payment, even though it was small. So did Rabia. Elham flew into a rage, but when I demanded they give back their portion if they didn't want to have it, she calmed down. The others, as in previous months, were content.

Again the moon shines full and I am greatly rejoicing. I found a fine herd of camels and bought many sound ones. Because of that herd, my earnings were forty-two pieces of silver. This month my wife and I have bought much-needed sandals and clothing. We've also dined well on meat and vegetables.

More than eight pieces of silver we've paid to our creditors. Even Elham didn't protest.

This plan is great because it leads us out of debt and gives us wealth that's ours to keep.

The moon had been full three times since I last carved upon this clay. Each time I paid myself one-tenth of all I earned. Each time my good wife and I have lived on seven-tenths even though at times it was difficult. Each time I have paid to my creditors two-tenths.

In my wallet, I now have twenty-one pieces of silver that are mine. I hold my head up high. It makes me proud to walk among my friends. My wife and I have made a happy home, and we are so glad to live together again.

The plan is invaluable. Look how it has made an honorable citizen out of a criminal.

~

TABLET NO. V

Again, the moon shines full, and I remember that it has been long since I carved the clay. Twelve moons have come and gone. But today, I won't neglect my record because today I have paid the last of my debts. This is the day when my wife and I celebrate with great feasting that our goal has been achieved.

Many things occurred on my final visit to my creditors that I will never forget. First, Ahmar begged my forgiveness for the unkind words and said that I was the one amongst all others most desired as a friend.

Old Elham isn't so bad after all, saying, "You were once a piece of soft clay to be pressed and molded by any hand that touched you, but now you are a piece of bronze capable of holding an edge. If you need silver or gold at any time, come to me."

Nor is she the only one who holds me in high regard. Many others speak respectfully to me. My wife also looks on me with a light in her eyes that gives me confidence in myself.

Yet it's the plan that has made my success. It has enabled me to pay all my debts and to jingle both gold and silver in my wallet. Therefore, I recommend it to anyone who wants to get ahead. If it can enable an ex-criminal to pay his debts and have gold in his wallet, it will help anyone find independence. And I'm not finished with it, because I am convinced that if I follow it further, it will make me rich in this city.

---------- Email Message ---------
From: Ellis Johnson <Ellis.Johnson@clearviewuniversity.org>
Date: Wed, July 21, 2021 at 3:30 PM
Subject: Re: Clay Tablets from Babylon?
To: Morgan Caldwell <Morgan.Caldwell@linwellmuseum.org>

HELLO AGAIN PROF. CALDWELL,

If, in your future rummaging in your vaults, or on a trip to those ruins of Babylon, you meet the ghost of a former resident, an old camel trader named Dabasir, do me a favor. Tell them that their scribbling on those clay tablets so long ago has earned them the life-long gratitude of a couple of folks back here in California.

You may remember me emailing you couple of years ago that my partner and I intended to try his plan for not only getting out of debt but also ending up with a little extra spending money in the end. You may have figured out, even though we tried to keep it from our friends, that we were actually in serious financial trouble.

We were kind of ashamed that we had some debts for years, and worried sick that our poor credit history might hurt my reputation and force me out of the college. We paid and paid – every cent we could squeeze out of our incomes – but it was barely enough to hold things together. It got so bad we were using debt from new credit cards to pay the debt from old credit at increasingly higher costs.

It developed into one of those vicious cycles that grows worse instead of better. Our struggles were getting hopeless. We couldn't move to a less expensive apartment because we owed the landlord. There didn't seem to be any way out of our predicament.

Then here comes your friend, the old camel trader from Babylon, with a plan to do just what we needed to accomplish, inspiring us to follow their system. So first, we made a list of all our debts, and I took it around and showed it to everyone we owed money to.

I explained how it was simply impossible for us to pay them off, the way things were going. They could easily see this themselves from the numbers. Then I explained that the only way I saw to pay in full was to set aside twenty percent of our income each month to be divided into equal parts, which would ultimately pay them all in full in a little over two years. In the meantime, we would live on a cash-only basis and buy things from them as well.

They were really quite decent about the whole thing. The manager at our grocery store put it best: "If you pay for all you buy and then pay some on what you owe, that's better than you have done, because you haven't paid anything on the account at all in three years."

Finally, I asked them all to sign an agreement binding them not to bother us or send our debts to a collection agency as long as twenty percent of our income was paid regularly. Then we began planning on how to live on seventy percent. We were determined to keep that extra ten percent to "jingle." The thought of having some savings was very enticing.

Making the change was like an adventure. We enjoyed figuring out different ways to live comfortably on that remaining seventy percent. We started with rent and managed to get a modest reduction from the landlord. Next, we took a close look at all of our expenses, from how we commuted to work to the brand of coffee we consumed. Always looking for ways to cut cost, without sacrificing our well-being and lifestyle too much.

It's too long a story for an email, but the short version is that it wasn't too difficult after all. We managed and enjoyed our new life-style too. What a relief it was to have our finances in such shape that we were no longer under the heavy burden of debt.

I have to tell you also about that extra ten percent we were supposed to "jingle." Well, we did jingle it for some time. Now don't laugh too soon: that was the fun part. We started accumulating money left over even after all our expenses were paid. There is more pleasure in running up such a surplus than there could be in spending it.

After we had "jingled our coins" to our hearts' content, we found a more profitable use for it – an investment that we could pay that ten percent into each month. This is proving to be the most satis-fying part of our financial makeover. It's the first thing we pay out of our income.

It's a really gratifying sense of security to know our investment is growing steadily. By the time my teaching days are over, it should be a comfortable sum, large enough so the income will take care of us from then on.

All this out of our same old income. Difficult to believe, yet totally true. All our debts are being gradually paid, and at the same time, our investment is increasing. Besides, we get along, financially, even better than before. Who would think there could be such a difference in results between following a financial plan and just drifting along.

At the end of next year, when all our old bills have been paid, we will have more to increase our contribution to our investment and have some extra for travel.

We are determined never again to let our living expenses exceed seventy percent of our income. Now you can understand why we would like to thank that old fellow whose plan saved us from our "Hell on Earth."

That camel trader knew. They had been through it all. They wanted others to benefit from their own bitter experiences. That's why they spent tedious hours carving their message on the clay. They had a real message for fellow sufferers, a message so important that after five thousand years, it has risen out of the ruins of Babylon, just as true and just as relevant as the day it was buried.

Thanks and best regards,

Ellis Johnson
Department of Archaeology
St. Catharine's College
Clearview University
Burleigh Hill, CA
Ellis.Johnson@clearviewuniversity.org

CHAPTER 10
THE LUCKIEST PERSON IN BABYLON

At the head of his caravan, Sharru Nada rode proudly, the merchant prince of Babylon. He liked fine cloth and wore rich and fashionable robes. He liked exotic animals and sat comfortably on his Arabian stallion. To look at him, one would hardly have guessed his age and many years. Indeed, they wouldn't have suspected that he was inwardly troubled.

The journey from Damascus is long, and the hardships of the desert many. The desert is also filled with fierce tribes eager to rob rich caravans like his. Yet Sharru wasn't concerned about any of these risks, because he employed mounted guards to provide protection.

What bothered him was the youth at his side. Hadan Gula, the grandson of his partner, Arad Gula, to whom he felt he owed a debt of gratitude that he could never repay. He wanted to do something for this grandson, but the more he considered it, the more difficult it seemed because of the youth himself.

Eyeing the young man's rings and earrings, he thought to himself, *He thinks wearing jewels is what wealth is all about, still he has his grandfather's strong face. But his grandfather wore no such gaudy robes. Yet, I asked him to join me, hoping I might help him get a start for himself and get away from the wreckage his father has made of their inheritance.*

Hadan Gula broke in on his thoughts. "Why do you work so hard, always riding with your caravan on its long journeys? Do you ever take time off to enjoy life?"

Sharru Nada smiled. "To enjoy life?" he repeated. "What would you do to enjoy life if you weren't traveling with me on this caravan?"

"If I had wealth equal to yours, I would live like a prince and never ride across the hot desert. I would spend the shekels as fast as they came to my wallet. I would wear the richest of robes and the rarest of jewels. That would be a life to my liking, a life worth living." Both laughed.

"Your grandfather wore no jewels." Sharru Nada spoke before he thought, then continued jokingly, "Would you leave any time for work?"

"Work is for servants and enslaved people," Hadan Gula responded.

Sharra Nada bit his lip and didn't reply, riding in silence until the trail led them to the slope. Here he reined his mount and pointed to the green valley far away. "See the valley there? Look far down and you will see the walls of Babylon in the distance. The tower you see is the Temple of Bel. If your eyes are sharp, you may even see the smoke from the eternal fire on its crest."

"So that is Babylon? I have always longed to see the wealthiest city in all the world," Hadan Gula commented. "Babylon, where my grandfather started his fortune. I wish he were still alive."

"Why do you wish his spirit to linger on earth beyond its allotted time? You and your father are more than capable of carrying on his legacy and work."

"Unfortunately, neither of us have his gifts. Father and I don't know his secret for attracting golden shekels."

Sharru Nada didn't reply but gave rein to his camel and rode thoughtfully down the trail to the valley. Behind them followed the caravan in a cloud of reddish dust. They reached the kings' highway and turned south through the irrigated farms.

Three older men plowing a field caught Sharru Nada's attention. They seemed strangely familiar. How ridiculous! After forty years, one doesn't pass a field and find the same men plowing there. Yet, something within him said they were the same. One, with an uncertain grip, held the plow. The other two plodded beside the oxen, ineffectually beating them with a stick to keep them pulling.

Forty years ago, he had envied these men! How gladly he would have exchanged places! But what a difference now. With pride, he looked back at his trailing caravan, well-chosen camels and donkeys loaded high with valuable goods from Damascus. And all this was just *some* of his possessions.

He pointed to the plowers, saying, "Still plowing the same field where they were forty years ago."

"They look it, but why do you think they are the same?"

"I saw them there," Sharru Nada replied. Memories were racing rapidly through his head. Why could he not bury the past and live in the present? Then he saw, as in a picture, the smiling face of Arad Gula. The barrier between himself and the cynical youth beside him dissolved.

But how could he help this young man with his spendthrift ideas and bejeweled hands? He could offer plenty of work to willing workers, but what could he offer to those who considered themselves too good for work? Yet he owed it to Arad Gula to do something, and not just a half-hearted attempt. He and Arad Gula had never done things that way. They weren't that sort of people.

A plan came almost in a flash — but there were objections. He must consider his own family and his position in the community. It would be cruel; it would hurt. But, being a man of quick decisions, he waved off the objections and decided to act.

"Would you be interested in hearing how your worthy grandfather and I joined in the partnership which proved so profitable?" he asked.

"Why not just tell me how you made the gold? That's all I need to know," the youth replied.

Sharru Nada ignored the answer and continued. "It starts with those men plowing. I was no older than you. As the column in which I marched approached, good old Megiddo, the farmer, scoffed at the slipshod way in which they plowed. Megiddo was chained next to me. 'Look at those lazy fellows,' he protested, 'the plow holder makes no effort to plow deep, nor do the beaters keep the oxen in the trench. How can they expect to raise a good crop with poor plowing?'"

"Did you say Megiddo was chained to you?" Hadan Gula asked in surprise.

"Yes, with bronze collars around our necks and a length of heavy chain between us. Next to him was Zabado, the sheep thief. I had known him in Harroun. At the end was a man we called Pirate because he never told us his name. We guessed that he was a sailor based on the entwined serpents tattooed on his chest in the sailor fashion. The column was made up like this so we could walk in fours."

"You were chained as criminals?" Hadan Gula asked incredulously.

"Didn't your grandfather tell you I was once enslaved?"

"He often spoke of you but never hinted about this."

"He was one you could trust with your innermost secrets. You, too, are also someone I can fully trust, right?" Sharru Nada looked him squarely in the eye.

"You may depend on my silence, but I am amazed. Tell me, how did you come to be enslaved?"

Sharru Nada shrugged his shoulders. "Anyone can find themselves a criminal and then be enslaved. It was a gambling house and barley beer that brought disaster to me. I was the victim of my brother's indiscretions. In a brawl, he injured a noble citizen. My parents were desperate to protect my brother from being prosecuted, because he worked and earned more than I did to provide for the family. And so they had me take the blame. I was bonded to the noble person's family by my parents. When my family couldn't raise the silver to free me, they sold me to the slave dealer."

"What a shame and injustice!" Hadan Gula protested. "But tell me, how did you regain freedom?"

"We will come to that, but not yet. Let me continue my tale. As we enslaved people continued our march, the plowers jeered at us. One did tip his ragged hat and bowed low, calling out, 'Welcome to Babylon, guests of the king. He waits for you on the city walls where the banquet is spread, mud bricks and onion soup.' With that, they laughed uproariously.

"Pirate flew into a rage and cursed them roundly. 'What do those farmers mean by the king awaiting us on the walls?' I asked him.

"'To the city walls, we march to carry bricks until our back breaks,' he replied. 'Or maybe they'll beat you so badly that you won't need to wait for your back to be broken.'

"Then Megiddo spoke up, 'It doesn't make sense to talk of guards and overseers beating willing, hard-working saves to death. Enslavers need obedient people to work. And if they work and work hard, they will treat them well enough.'

"'Who wants to work hard?' commented Zabado. 'Those plowers are wise fellows. They're not breaking their backs working hard. They just pretend they do.'

"'You can't get ahead by laziness,' Megiddo protested. 'If you plow a hectare, that's a good day's work, and anyone, enslaver, an enslaved person, or laborer, knows it. But when you plow only half as much, that's laziness. I am not lazy. I like to work, and I like to do good work, because work is the best friend I've ever known. It has brought me all the good things I've had, my farm and cows and crops – everything.'

"'Yes, and where are these things now?' scoffed Zabado. 'I figure it pays better to be smart and get by without working. Watch me if we're brought to the walls to work. I'll be carrying the water bag or some easy job when you, who like to work, will be breaking your back carrying bricks.' He laughed his silly laugh.

"Terror gripped me that night. I couldn't sleep. I crowded close to the guard rope, and when the others slept, I attracted the attention of Godoso, who was doing the first guard watch.

"'Tell me, Godoso,' I whispered, 'when we get to Babylon, will we be brought to the walls?'

"'Why do you want to know?' they questioned cautiously.

"'Do you not understand?' I pleaded. 'I am young. I want to live. I don't want to be worked or beaten to death on the walls. Is there any chance for me to get a good master?'

"They whispered back. 'I will tell you something. You are a good fellow. You have given me no trouble. We will first go to the slave market when we get to the city. Listen to me. When buyers come, tell them you are a good worker. Tell them you like to work hard for a good master. Make them want to buy you. If you don't make them buy you, the next day you will be at the wall, carrying bricks. Back-breaking work.'

"After he walked away, I lay in the warm sand, looking up at the stars and thinking about work. What Megiddo had said about it being his best friend made me wonder if it would be my best friend as well. Certainly, it would be if it helped me out of this.

"When Megiddo awoke, I whispered my good news to him. It was our one ray of hope as we marched toward Babylon. Then, late in the afternoon, we approached the walls and could see the lines of people, like black ants, climbing up and down the steep diagonal paths. As we drew closer, we were amazed at the thousands of workers. Some were digging in the moat; others mixed the dirt into mud bricks. Most carried bricks in large baskets up those steep trails to the masons.

"Overseers cursed the slow ones and cracked whips over the backs of those who failed to keep in line. Poor worn-out souls were seen to stagger and fall beneath their heavy baskets, unable to rise again. If the whip couldn't bring them to their feet, they were pushed to the side of the paths and left writhing in agony. Soon they would be dragged down to join other broken bodies beside the roadway to await their fate. As I looked at the dreadful sight, I shuddered. So this was what awaited my father's son if he failed at the slave market.

"Godoso had been right. We were taken through the city's gates to the central prison and marched to the pens in the market the following day. Here the rest of the prisoners huddled in fear, and only the whips of our guard could keep them moving so the buyers could examine them. Megiddo and I eagerly talked to every buyer who permitted us to address them.

"The slave-dealer brought soldiers from the king's guard who shackled Pirate and beat him brutally when he protested. I felt sorry for him as he was led away.

"Megiddo felt that we would soon part. When no buyers were near, he talked to me earnestly to impress upon me how valuable work would be to me in the future: 'Some hate it. They make it their enemy. Better to treat it like a friend, make yourself like it. Never mind if it's hard. If you think you will build a good home, who cares if the beams you must carry are heavy? Promise me, if you get a master, work for them as hard as you can. If they don't appreciate all you do, don't worry about it. Remember, work, well done, is good for the person who does it. It makes you a better person.' He stopped as a stocky farmer came to the enclosure and looked at us critically.

"Megiddo asked about her farm and crops, soon convincing her that he would be a valuable addition. After vigorous bargaining with the slave dealer, the farmer pulled out a fat purse from beneath her robe, and soon Megiddo had followed this farmer out of sight.

"A few others were sold during the morning. At noon Godoso confided to me that the dealer was unhappy and wouldn't stay in the city for another night but instead would take all who remained unsold at sundown to the king's buyer. I was becoming desperate when a good-natured person walked up to the wall and inquired if a baker was among us.

"I approached them saying, 'Why should a good baker like yourself seek an inferior baker to join them? Wouldn't it be easier to teach your skilled ways to a willing person like me? Look at me. I am young, strong, and like to work. Give me a chance, and I will do my best to earn gold and silver for you.'

"They were impressed by my willingness and began bargaining with the dealer who had never noticed me since he had bought me but now couldn't stop expounding on my abilities, good health, and good disposition. I felt like an animal being sold to a butcher. At last, much to my joy, the deal was closed. I followed my new master away, thinking I was the luckiest person in Babylon.

"My new home was much to my liking. Nana-naid, my master, taught me how to grind the barley in the stone bowl that stood in the courtyard and build a fire in the oven. They also showed me how to grind the sesame flour for the honey cakes finely. I had a couch in the shed where the grain was stored. The old housekeeper, Swasti, fed me well and was pleased how I helped her with the heavy tasks.

"Here was the chance I had longed for to make myself valuable to my master and, I hoped, find a way to earn my freedom.

"I asked Nana-naid to show me how to knead the bread and to bake, and they did, very pleased at my willingness. Later, when I could do this well, I asked them to show me how to make the honey cakes, and soon I was doing all the baking. My master was glad to be idle, but Swasti shook her head in disapproval, 'No work to do is bad for anyone,' she declared.

"I felt it was time for me to think of a way by which I might start to earn coins to buy my freedom. As the baking was finished at noon, I thought Nana-naid would approve if I found profitable employment for the afternoons and might share my earnings with me. Then the thought came to me, *Why not bake more of the honey cakes and sell them to hungry people on the city streets?*

"I presented my plan to Nana-naid this way: 'If I can use my afternoons after the baking is finished to earn you coins, would it be fair for you to share the earnings with me so that I might have money of my own to spend on those things which everyone desires and needs?'

"'Fair enough, fair enough,' they admitted. So when I told them of my plan to sell our honey cakes, they were pleased. 'Here is what we will do,' they suggested. 'You sell them at two for a penny, then half of the pennies will be mine to pay for the flour and the honey and the wood to bake them. Of the rest, I'll take half, and you keep half.'

"I was pleased by this offer allowing me to keep one-fourth of my sales for myself. That night I worked late to make a tray to display the cakes. Nana-naid gave me one of their worn robes so that I would look presentable, and Swasti helped me patch it and wash it clean.

"The next day, I baked an extra supply of honey cakes. They looked brown and tempting on the tray. I went along the street, shouting loudly. At first, no one seemed interested, and I started to become discouraged. But I kept on, and later in the afternoon, as people became hungry, the cakes began to sell and soon my tray was empty.

"Nana-naid was pleased with my success and gladly paid me my share. I was delighted to own pennies. Megiddo had been right when he said a master appreciated good work. That night I was so excited over my success I could hardly sleep and tried to figure out how much I could earn in a year and how many years would be required to buy my freedom.

"As I went out with my tray of cakes every day, I soon found regular customers. One of these was none other than your grandfather, Arad Gula. He was a rug merchant. Going from one end of the city to the other, he sold his rugs, accompanied by a donkey loaded high with rugs and an enslaved person to tend it. He would buy two cakes for himself and two for his enslaved servant, always lingering to talk with me while they ate their cakes.

"Your grandfather said something to me one day that I will never forget. 'I like your cakes, but I like the promising enterprise with which you offer them even more. That kind of spirit will carry you far on the road to success.'

"But how can you understand, Hadan Gula, what such words of encouragement could mean to an enslaved person, lonesome in a great city, struggling with all he had in him to find a way out of his humiliation?

"As the months went by, I continued to add pennies to my wallet. It began to have a comforting weight on my belt. Work was proving to be my best friend, just as Megiddo had said. I was happy, but Swasti was worried.

"'I fear your master spends too much time at the gaming houses,' she protested.

"I was overjoyed one day to meet my friend Megiddo on the street. He was leading three donkeys loaded with vegetables to the market. 'I am doing very well,' he said. 'My master appreciates my good work. I am now a foreman. She trusts me to sell her products, and she is also sending for my family. Work is helping me to recover from my great trouble. Someday it will help me buy my freedom and once more own a farm of my own.'

"Time went on, and Nana-naid became more and more anxious for me to return from selling. They would be waiting when I returned and would eagerly count and divide our money. Nana-naid would also urge me to seek other markets and increase my sales.

"Often, I went outside the city gates to sell to the overseers of the enslaved people building the walls. I hated to return to the unpleasant sights but found the overseers good buyers of my cakes. One day I was surprised to see Zabado, the sheep thief, waiting in line to fill his basket with bricks. He was thin and bent, and his back was covered with welts and sores from the overseers' whips. I was sorry for him and handed him a cake. He stuff it into his mouth like a hungry animal. Seeing the greedy look in his eyes, I ran before he could grab my tray.

"'Why did you work so hard?' Arad Gula said to me one day. 'Almost the same question you asked of me today, do you remember?' I told him what Megiddo had said about work and how it proved to be my best friend. I showed him my wallet of pennies with pride and explained how I was saving them to buy my freedom.

"'When you are free, what will you do?' he inquired.

"'Then,' I answered, 'I intend to become a merchant.'

"Hearing that, he confided in me – something I had never suspected. 'You didn't, couldn't know, but I am also enslaved. I am in partnership with my master.'"

"'Stop,'" demanded Hadan Gula. 'I won't listen to lies smearing my grandfather's good name. He wasn't enslaved.' His eyes blazed in anger.

"Sharru Nada remained calm. 'I honor him for rising above his misfortune and becoming a leading citizen of Damascus. Are you, his grandson, cast from the same mold? Are you mature enough to face facts, or are you still a child who would prefer to believe in false tales?'

"Hadan Gula straightened in his saddle. Then, in a voice suppressed with deep emotion, he replied, 'My grandfather was beloved by all. He performed countless good deeds. When the famine came, was it not his gold that he used to buy grain in Egypt. Was it not his caravan that brought it to Damascus and distributed it to the people so no one would starve? Now you say he was despised and enslaved in Babylon.'

"'Had he remained enslaved in Babylon, then he might very well have been despised. But when, through his efforts, he became a great citizen in Damascus, the Gods indeed condoned his misfortunes and honored him with their respect,' Sharru Nada replied.

"After telling me that he was enslaved, Sharru Nada continued. He explained how anxious he had been to earn his freedom. However, now that he had enough money to buy this, he was much disturbed about what he should do. His sales had slowed, and he feared to leave the support of his master.

"I protested his indecision: 'Don't cling to your master. Be free again. Act like a free person and succeed like one! Decide what you desire to accomplish, and then work will help you to achieve it!' He went on his way, saying he was glad I had scolded him for his cowardice.

"One day, as I went outside the gates, I was surprised to find a great crowd gathering there. When I asked for an explanation, someone replied: 'Have you not heard? An escaped enslaved person who injured one of the king's guards has been brought to justice and will be publicly beaten for his crime today. Even the king will be here.'

"The crowd was so dense I feared to go near, as I didn't want my tray of honey cakes to tip. So I climbed up the unfinished wall to see over the heads of the people. I was fortunate to have a view of the great king himself as he rode by in his golden chariot. Never had I beheld such grandeur, such robes, and hangings of gold cloth and velvet.

"I couldn't see the beating though I could hear the screams of the poor enslaved person. I wondered how one so noble as our king could endure seeing such suffering. Yet when I saw he was laughing and joking with his nobles, I knew he was cruel and understood why he could demand such inhuman tasks of the enslaved people building the walls.

"After the enslaved man was beaten, he was left to suffer in the public square. He was left there, so all might see what befalls those who challenge the kings and his laws. As the crowd began to thin, I could see the beaten body. On the enslaved man's chest, I saw tattooed, two entwined serpents. It was Pirate.

"The next time I met Arad Gula, he was a changed man. He greeted me full of enthusiasm: 'Behold, the enslaved man you knew is now free. There was magic in those words. Already my sales and my profits are increasing. I have met and married my wife. She is the niece of my old master and is thrilled with my success. She wants us to move to a different city where no one will know I was once enslaved. That way, our children will be above any shame they might feel for their father's youthful misdeeds. Work has become my best helper. It has enabled me to recapture my confidence and my skill to sell.'

"I was delighted that I had been able, even in a small way, to repay him for the encouragement he had given me.

"One evening, Swasti came to me in deep distress: 'Our master is in trouble. I fear for them. Some months ago, they lost a lot of money at the gaming tables. Nana-naid hasn't paid the farmer for the grain or honey. Nana-naid hasn't paid the moneylender. The moneylender and farmer are angry and have threatened them.'

"'Why should we worry about Nana-naid's foolishness. We aren't their parents,' I replied thoughtlessly.

"'Foolish youth, you don't understand. What do you think Nana-naid gave to the moneylender to secure their loan? Your title. You will belong to the lender if they don't pay. What would a money-lender need of a baker? The lender is sure to sell you. I didn't want to be sold. Nana-naid is a good master. Why? Why would such trouble come upon them?'

"Swasti's fears were justified. While I was baking the following day, the moneylender returned with someone called Sasi, who looked me over and said I would do.

"The moneylender didn't even wait for my master to return but told Swasti to tell Nana-naid they had taken me. Then, with only the robe on my back and the sack of pennies hanging safely from my belt, I pulled away from my oven.

"I was whirled away from my dearest hopes like a hurricane snatches the tree from the forest and casts it into the surging sea. Again gambling houses and barley beer had caused me disaster.

"Sasi was a blunt and gruff. As I was led across the city, I told Sasi of the excellent work I had been doing for Nana-naid and said I hoped to do good work for them. Their reply offered no encouragement.

'What do I care about baking? I don't need or want a baker. I have been charged with building a section of the Grand Canal for the king. I need workers. You will work to build it, not bake it.'

"Picture a desert with not a tree, just low shrubs and a sun burning with such fury the water in our barrels became so hot we could scarcely drink it. Then picture rows of people going down into the deep pit and lugging heavy baskets of dirt up soft, dusty trails from daylight until dark. Picture food served in open troughs from which we helped ourselves like pigs. We had no tents, no straw for beds. That was the situation in which I found myself. I buried my wallet in a marked spot, wondering if I would ever dig it up again.

"At first, I worked with goodwill, but as the months dragged on, I felt my spirit breaking. Then the heat fever took hold of my weary body. I lost my appetite and could scarcely eat the terrible food we were given. At night I would toss in unhappy wakefulness.

"In my misery, I wondered if Zabado had the best plan, to shirk work to keep his back from being broken. Then I recalled my last sight of him and knew his plan wasn't a good one.

"I thought of Pirate and wondered if it might be just as well to fight and try to escape. However, the memory of his broken body reminded me that his plan was also useless.

Then I remembered my last sight of Megiddo. His hands were worn and calloused from hard work, but his heart was light, and there was happiness on his face. His was the best plan.

"I was just as willing to work as Megiddo; he couldn't have worked harder than I did. So why didn't my work bring me happiness and success? Was it work that brought Megiddo happiness, or was it just an accident of luck? Was I to work the rest of my life without gaining my desires, without joy and success? All of these questions were jumbled in my mind, and I had no answers. Indeed, I was baffled. Several days later, when it seemed that my body was going to give out, I was ordered to leave the pit. A messenger had come from my master to take me back to Babylon. I dug up my precious wallet, wrapped myself in the tattered remnants of my robe, and was on my way.

"As we rode, the same thoughts of a hurricane whirling me here and there kept racing through my head. "Was it my destiny to be punished for the rest of my life? If so, why me? Why did I deserve to be treated this way? What new miseries and disappointments awaited me?

"When we rode to the courtyard of my master's house, you can imagine my surprise when I saw Arad Gula waiting for me. He helped me down and hugged me like a long-lost brother.

"As we went our way, I would normally have followed him as the enslaved must follow their enslaver, but he wouldn't permit me. He put his arm around me, saying, 'I searched everywhere for you. When I had almost given up hope, I met Swasti, who told me of the moneylender, who directed me to your noble owner. He drove a hard bargain and made me pay an outrageous price, but you are worth it.

Your way of thinking and your ability to work and earn have been my inspiration to this new success.'

"'Megiddo's philosophy, not mine,' I interrupted.

"'Megiddo's and you. Thanks to you both, we are going to Damascus, and I need you as my partner. In a moment, you will be a free man!' So saying he drew from beneath his robe the clay tablet carrying my title, raised it above his head, and hurled it to break in a hundred pieces on the cobblestones. Then, he stamped on the pieces with glee until they were dust.

"Tears of gratitude filled my eyes. I knew I was the luckiest person in Babylon.

"'In the time of my greatest distress, work proved to be my best friend. My willingness to work enabled me to escape being sold and join the enslaved people on the walls. It also so impressed your grandfather that he selected me for his partner.'

"Then Hadan Gula questioned, 'Was work my grandfather's secret key to the golden shekels?'

"'It was the only key he had when I knew him,' Sharru Nada replied. "'Your grandfather enjoyed working. The gods appreciated his efforts and rewarded him greatly.'

"'I'm starting to see,' Hadan Gula said thoughtfully. 'Work attracted his many friends who admired his industry and the success it brought. Work brought him the honors he enjoyed so much in Damascus. Work brought him all those things I have wanted for myself. And I thought work was fit only for enslaved people and servants.'

"'Life is rich with many pleasures for people to enjoy,' Sharru Nada commented. 'Each has its place. I am glad that work isn't reserved for the enslaved and servants. If that were the case, I would be deprived of my greatest pleasure. Many things I enjoy, but nothing takes the place of work.'

"Sharru Nada and Hadan Gula rode in the shadows of the towering walls up to Babylon's massive bronze gates. The gate guards jumped to attention and respectfully saluted an honored citizen at his approach. Then, with head held high, Sharru Nada led the long caravan through the gates and up the city's streets.

"'I have always hoped to be like my grandfather,'" Hadan Gula confided to him. 'I never realized just what kind of person he was. You have shown me. Now that I understand, I admire him even more and feel more determined to be like him. I fear I can never repay you for giving me the true key to his success. From this day forth, I shall use his key. I will start as humbly as he started.'

"So saying, Hadan Gula pulled the jeweled baubles from his ears and the rings from his fingers. Then, reining his horse, he dropped back and rode behind the caravan leader with deep respect."

THANK YOU

Thank you for reading this revised version of *The Richest ~~Man~~ Person In Babylon.* Please consider leaving a review on your preferred online bookstore if you enjoyed it. A review can help people like you find this valuable resource.

If you know anyone who may benefit from reading this version of *The Richest ~~Man~~ Person in Babylon,* it would mean the world to me if you recommend it to them.

Also, bulk discounts are available for orders of 10 copies or more. With your help, we can get this updated and inclusive version into more hands and onto more library shelves. Contact info@patterin.com for more information.

ABOUT THE AUTHOR

George Samuel Clason was born in Louisiana, Missouri, on November 7, 1874. He attended the University of Nebraska and served in the United States Army during the Spanish–American War. Beginning a long career in publishing, he founded the Clason Map Company of Denver, Colorado, and published the first road atlas of the United States and Canada. In 1926, he issued the first of a famous series of pamphlets on thrift and financial success, using parables set in ancient Babylon to make each of his points.

These were distributed in large quantities by banks and insurance companies and became familiar to millions, the most famous being *"The Richest Man in Babylon,"* the parable from which the present volume takes its title. These "Babylonian parables" have become a modern inspirational classic.

ABOUT THE EDITORS

Clifton D. Corbin, MBA, PMP, was a business consultant with over two decades of experience when he left the office to become a full-time stay-at-home dad of two. *The Richest Man in Babylon* has held a special place in his heart since reading it as a young adult. The book inspired Clifton to study economics and personal finance. After attempting to read the original version to his son, he realized it could use a 21st century refresher.

Corbin is the author of *Your Kids, Their Money: A Parent's Guide To Raising Financially Literate Children*, which provides parents with the skills and tools to teach financial literacy to their children. He is a passionate advocate for advancing the financial literacy of children and adults.

Kaleb K. A. Corbin is an outgoing and money curious soul. He has spent his early years learning how to acquire money to grow his Pokémon card collection. He has been the tester of many of his father's money analogizes, worksheets and projects.

In 2022 he took his first steps into investing, buying his first investment, an S&P index ETF. He continues to seek information on how to earn, secure what he has and save and invest for his future.

linkedin.com/in/cdcorbin

twitter.com/cdcorbin

instagram.com/yourkidstheirmoney

ALSO BY PATTERIN PUBLISHING

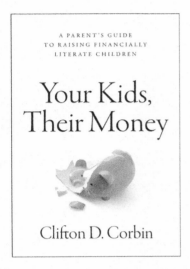

A PARENT'S GUIDE
TO RAISING FINANCIALLY
LITERATE CHILDREN

Your Kids,
Their Money

Clifton D. Corbin

Your Kids, Their Money gives you the tools to teach your children about the one area many parents never talk about - money.

Your Kids, Their Money is the clear and simple guide you need to help teach financial literacy to your children. Applicable for kids of all ages, this guide is an investment you will want to make in building a solid foundation for your children's future.

Drawing on his master's in business administration (MBA), finance experience, and practices with his own children, Clifton Corbin provides a guide for the modern parent. In this book you will learn how to educate your children on the basics of money management such as allowances and first jobs, borrowing, credit, and investing, in ways that make sense to parents and appeal to kids.

Clifton's innovative approach starts by identifying teachable moments during everyday activities. You will see how to involve children in the family's finances, showing them where money comes from, how to save more, and why it's essential for kids to understand why sometimes you just can't afford some things. Throughout the book are activities and games that you and your kids can participate in to learn even more.

Made in United States
North Haven, CT
27 February 2023

33254197R00093